C0-CDH-429

# The New Products Workshop

## Hands-On Tools for Developing Winners

Barry Feig

McGraw-Hill, Inc.
New York St. Louis San Francisco Auckland Bogotá
Caracas Lisbon London Madrid Mexico Milan
Montreal New Delhi Paris San Juan São Paulo
Singapore Sydney Tokyo Toronto

Library of Congress Cataloging-in-Publication Data

Feig, Barry.
The new products workshop : hands-on tools for developing winners / Barry Feig.
p. cm.
ISBN 0-07-020351-2
1. New products. I. Title.
HF5415.153.F34 1993
658.5'75—dc20 92-30202
CIP

This book is printed on recycled, acid-free paper containing a minimum of 50% recycled de-inked fiber.



1 2 3 4 5 6 7 8 9 0 DOC/DOC 9 8 7 6 5 4 3 2

ISBN 0-07-020351-2

*The sponsoring editor for this book was Karen Hansen, the editing supervisor was Stephen M. Smith, and the production supervisor was Suzanne W. Babeuf. It was set in Palatino by McGraw-Hill's Professional Book Group composition unit.*

*Printed and bound by R. R. Donnelley & Sons Company.*

*This book is dedicated to my wife, Nancy,*
*who taught me how to write;*
*my children, Meredith and Jeremy,*
*who continually teach me how to think;*
*and my mom and dad (and brother and sister), who still don't know what I do for a living and think I'm crazy but love me anyway*

# Contents

# Preface

Being an entrepreneur and creating a successful new product has become part of the great American Dream. Unlike many dreams, this one is attainable. Success can happen at any time, at any age. In the new-product world, little matters as long as you can satisfy the consumer.

Ideas are free. Everyone seems to have the next great new-product idea...if only they could market it. The world is saturated with that famous dinner party refrain, "I thought of that first...I could have made millions."

New-product development is also crucial to the ongoing success of existing businesses, for such development ensures a company's future and vitality. Few things conquer corporate rigor mortis and invigorate morale better than a hot new product or a steady stream of new-product introductions.

This book is about developing new products that succeed and about marketing them creatively.

The book is aimed at three levels:

- The entrepreneur or company manager who wants to launch a new product or new-product program (where an idea may or may not exist)
- The entrepreneur or company manager who has a new product and says, "Now what?"
- The company that wants to vitalize or position an existing product, concept, or service.

Writing this book has been an excellent exercise for me. It made me relearn what I have been telling others to do over the years as both a strategist or think tank for new products and positionings, and through my articles. Even experienced marketers, who think they know their business and markets thoroughly, should take the time to relearn the basics that we tend to forget in the day-to-day operations of our business. As I am constantly reminded, even .300 hitters take batting lessons.

Whether you're a manager trying to enter a new business, an entrepreneur trying to enter a new market, or a new-products manager for a large company, new-product development can be an exciting and rewarding, albeit stressful and daunting, experience.

Introducing or developing a new product takes a different knowledge base than running an existing business. Contrary to what we'd like to believe, new products don't spring forth fully grown from the new-product patch. They are slowly nurtured and grown to maturity. Also, as we undoubtedly know, making the best product does not necessarily mean the best-selling product.

This book is about how to make the most of the fragile sequence when a manager or entrepreneur first plots a new-product project and strives to turn an idea into reality. Hopefully, the many examples I mention, all real, can be adapted for your particular marketing situation. They should at least serve as idea-joggers to spur you on to new thinking or point out areas to avoid.

The book establishes several new principles that go far beyond the scope of the typical business school coursework. Each chapter stands on its own. But, like the new-product development process itself, each chapter may impact another. I suggest you read Chaps. 1 through 6 as a unit before taking the marketing steps proposed.

The chapters on positioning and "share of heart" are two keys for winning the hearts and minds of consumers. The work flow spelled out in Chap. 6 recaps the workshop process in detail, with time frames to aid you in planning.

Each chapter is followed by the questions (and answers) I get asked most often at presentations and business meetings. These questions and answers also serve to summarize the chapter. Most chapters also have a how-to section with suggestions on implementing the program.

The methods in this book have evolved over more than two decades. They're proven. Our approach has created and identified over $2 billion in sales in such diverse industries as beverages, financial services, heavy equipment, cosmetics, and over-the-counter drugs. If we do not include your business category specifically, the principles remain the same. You still have to fulfill a need of some kind.

If you're an entrepreneur, I have attempted to treat your funds as if they were my own. Having a big budget and scads of backers may even be a negative. When money is scarce, one must work smarter.

If you work for a larger company, I have tried to streamline the new-product process, taking advantage of all your available resources in the quickest, most efficient way possible.

If you already have a product, I suggest you take a step back and use the information in the book to refine your product or distribution strategy and get an additional reality check. New-product development involves sleepless nights, moments of euphoria, hours of self-doubt, and scads of decisions, every one of which will impact another. New-product development is an intensely speculative, labor-intensive discipline. On the surface, the odds against major success seem tough. In fact, mortgaging the house and putting the proceeds on red at the roulette wheel seems to be the more secure investment.

But the odds are overcome every day by people who know and understand that consumers drive the new-product business. The rewards for the 25-hour days and 50-hour weekends can be great. And long lived. Swanson's frozen dinners have outlasted eight presidents, a cold war...even the Soviet Republic.

To consumers, the only thing that is important is the one thing that all successful new products have in common: They solve a human being's latent or existing desire. Despite the universe of new products, there are enough unfilled consumer needs—and marketing opportunities—to last for many more centuries.

*Barry Feig*

# 1
# User-Oriented Product Development

*Chapter preview:*

- ***What user-oriented product development is***
- ***The difference between a feature and a benefit and why it's vital to your new-product success***
- ***Making money on wants and needs***
- ***Why new products are big news to most Americans***
- ***Types of new products***
- ***Why breakthrough new products are almost never an immediate success***
- ***How to adapt and adopt to bring a successful new product to market***
- ***Turning the odds for success in your favor***
- ***Why most new products fail***
- ***What the consumer cares and doesn't care about***

Way back in the early twentieth century, George Eastman, the marketer of the first successful camera and Kodak's founder, called his sales force to a meeting:

"What are we selling?" he asked.

"Pictures," said one salesperson.

"Cameras, good ones!" called out another.

"Film," said yet another.

"You're all wrong," said Eastman. "We're selling none of these. Our product is memories. That's what the customer is buying."

Eastman was developing his products from the consumer's point of view. George Eastman knew that the customer (or as we say in today's jargon, the consumer) is the real world and the only thing that matters. He also knew that his camera was only a tool—a piece of hardware. The visions of times past—those wisps of images and frozen movement locked forever onto something we could hold in our hands and look at whenever we wanted—were the real purchase motivators.

Solutions and benefits are what move people to buy. That was

Eastman's message. That's the thread that runs through all successful new-product development and throughout this book.

People don't buy products.

They don't buy features.

They buy benefits.

As the people from Black & Decker remind us, people don't want 1/4-inch drill bits, they want 1/4-inch holes. This may sound basic, but only if, like most people, you think of a benefit as something tangible, as something only capable of being held and touched. A benefit can also be a feeling or an emotional kick—sort of a pep rally for the mind.

This book is about developing products driven by the consumer and the nuances of the marketplace. When we use the word *consumer,* we're referring to industrial consumers as well as mass market consumers.

When we refer to a *new product,* we'll define it as a product (or service) you have not sold before. It might not have even existed before in any shape or form, although this is rather unlikely.

New-product development is not what you would call an exact science. Dealing with something as quixotic and mercurial as a human mind never can be. But new-product development can be handled scientifically, through trial and error, when we take the time and the necessary steps to get it right. Risks are always going to be involved, but we can take them knowledgeably and creatively. Our approach is proactive—not reactive. And actionable.

But why develop new products at all? Surely, all basic consumer needs have been met. For the most part, consumers are reasonably satisfied with currently available products. Who needs yet another new product when we haven't figured out what to do with the physical remains and skeletons of our old ones yet?

You do. And the consumer does. New products are vital to businesses. They help keep your company young and one step ahead of the competition. New products are great for morale too, since everyone feels a part of new-product birthing and success.

But it's more than that. Developing a successful new product is about human achievement, and possibly, if you're an entrepreneur, about becoming financially independent. The new-product fantasy is about hitting it big, where the Great American Dream can unfold before your eyes. It's also about presenting a moving target to your competitors so they never know quite what they're up against and stay constantly off guard.

Successful new-product development is about transcending your life's experiences and getting into your neighbor's head. Or getting into the head of someone you have never seen or heard of before, but who may exist a thousand miles or more away.

New products are news to the consumers. Dramatic news. People actually want to try your product. Americans adore new products. Stumbling over new pleasures and ways to make life simpler or more pleasurable are some of the nicer things about being human. But consumers won't make a judgment about a product until someone shows them why it would make life simpler or more pleasurable. *Consumers don't spend time thinking about new products. They simply react to what's put in front of them.*

## Some Basics

All successful new products start and end with consumers buying something they want or need. Wants create needs. For instance, the world was not waiting for a new electronic game when the Nintendo Entertainment System was introduced. But the game spread as kids saw the enjoyment potential, which created a want.

As the game spread, a bandwagon effect took place. All the kids on the block wanted the game—and they wanted it oh so desperately. The want was converted to an emotional need. (See Fig. 1-1.)

In short, the introduction of the Nintendo system created a whole chain of events that led to a need being generated. But this vital process started long before the Nintendo system hit the market. Nintendo invested time and money in research before it was launched. The system didn't just magically appear. Someone at Nintendo had the dream and the desire to turn that dream into a reality.

Talking about the necessities of learning about your market and discovering (and fulfilling) consumer needs as a key to success reeks of Marketing 101. These principles sound rather simplistic but get forgotten as you strive to bring a product to fruition.

In many corporate new-product programs, the act of following the new-product development plan, and the politics involved, often takes on greater significance than the product itself. The product becomes sort of the by-product of the new-product development function. That's counterproductive.

*Entrepreneurs tend to get caught up in the syndrome of trying to make what they prefer rather than what the consumer wants.* Entrepreneurs tend to believe only what they have encountered and have had reinforced in their personal experience. Their preconceived notions lead them to false starts—or, more disastrously—expensive product failures. It's better to at least start the right way and play the odds rather than work against them.

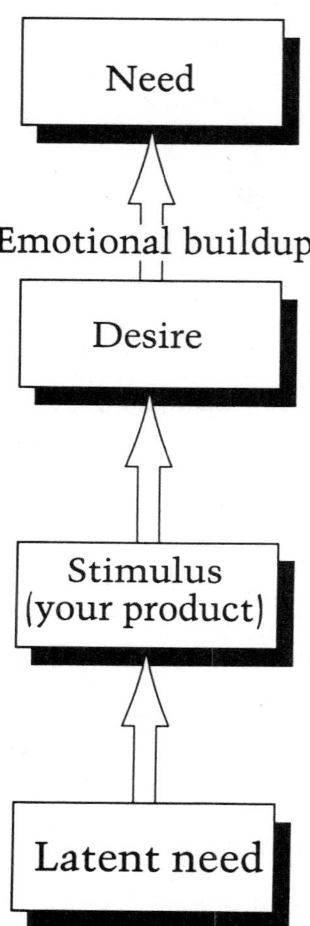


**Figure 1-1.** How a stimulus (your product) brings a latent need to the surface.

## The Workshop Fundamentals

The path to creating a successful new product is rarely a linear affair. Like a movie, developing a successful new product is a series of evolving, sequential events. Successful development involves plot twists, your own unique cast of characters, and a few red herrings thrown in for good measure. The key words are to creatively *adapt* and *adopt* and to sell what's selling. Adapt your ideas, technologies, and resources to ever-changing consumer needs. Adopt the most promising positioning to deliver these needs. And expose these products and positionings to consumers and the trade to make sure you're getting it right. New ideas, new research, prior and ongoing failures, even serendipitous events can be managed, planned, and built upon when you remember these key words:

The Consumer, First and Foremost

Here are some marketing facts that may surprise you:

George Eastman did not invent the camera, he was simply a master in simplifying the picture-taking process so that everyone could take pictures and afford to get them developed.

Thomas Edison didn't invent today's electrical network. His talent was in marketing it. At one time he was in a hotly contested duel with George Westinghouse, and Edison merely marketed his AC system better than Westinghouse marketed his DC system.

Henry Ford didn't invent the car. He wasn't even trying to build his now-famous assembly-line. He simply recognized that consumers would buy a car for $500 if someone could make them that cheap. The assembly-line process for which he became famous was actually a by-product. The car was one of our first truly mass-produced consumer-driven products (pun definitely intended).

These people knew, and smart marketers know, that instead of making the consumer change behavior and spending patterns to adapt to a new breakthrough, the marketer must adapt to the consumer and learn the consumer's thought processes. That's one of the key factors to new-product success.

Another major factor that should go into a new-product program but rarely does is the use and encouragement of the "happy accident," as my friend and fellow new-product developer Ernest Potischman likes to call it. Breakthroughs and dynamic successes often result from unexpected events—from the discovery of penicillin to the placing of Arm & Hammer baking soda in the refrigerator. These moments of eureka can and will happen at any given moment when we set the stage and don't allow the rigidity of our thought processes and preconceived notions to get in our way.

Identifying and then fulfilling a consumer need is much more effective and less expensive, in terms of money, time, and reputations, than the more traditional corporate, "We made it, now you sell it" multidepartment approach to new-product development. Of course, many products were driven by engineering and have worked out, but almost every company has an expansive archive of products that looked truly marvelous to marketers and engineers but were greeted by consumers with turned-down thumbs.

When you fail to identify the product opportunity ahead of time in terms of the consumer's wants or needs or don't learn about the emotions that will drive your product, you are merely guessing about your product's acceptance. With the new-product failure rate at around 85 percent, why risk guessing?

## Types of New Products

Most people tend to think of a new product as a radically new type of invention. Inventors and research and development departments (R&D) love these, but they are the riskiest ventures of all. Rarely are dramatic new products successful. Most truly successful new products are adaptations of something that already exists. (See Table 1-1.) For instance, power hand tools were once made almost exclusively of metal, but plastic's lighter weight and lack of electrical conductivity has made it the material of choice.

*A new product can be a real breakthrough product—a totally new and different idea.* It can change the way we do the most ordinary of tasks, as did automatic teller machines and microwaves. These advances are rare and risky. Statistics are always a bit iffy, but a survey in an industry trade paper says this category is where the greatest ultimate profits are—but only if you have the fortitude and staying power to make it work. The technology for the microwave oven, for example, has actually been around since the early 1940s. It took almost 40 years of marketing and development to get microwave ovens in a substantial portion of people's homes. Even today's computers are based on technologies that were available almost half a century ago.

The word *innovation* means different things to different people. One scientist's innovation may be another's "So what?" Innovation just for the sake of innovation is fun and challenging but usually profitless.

Consumers tend to be wary of radical new ideas. A big drawback of the breakthrough new product is that consumers have to figure out how the product fits into their lives—whether it's really worth it in terms of money and bother. More than one product has failed because its time had not yet come or the concept was too difficult to sell to the ultimate consumer. Some examples were the quadraphonic stereos of some years back and the original Panasonic TV/VCR combo (actually introduced in the 1970s) which was eventually simplified and evolved into today's videocassette recorder.

**Table 1-1.** Where Are the New-Product Opportunities?

| Product type | Advantages | Disadvantages | Examples |
|---|---|---|---|
| True break-through | High profit | High failure rate<br>High R&D expense | Epilady hair remover<br>Betamax VCR<br>Selectavision by RCA<br>Lactaid (enzyme for breaking down milk sugar) |
| Adaptations of existing product | Greater chance of success<br>More predictable sales patterns<br>Low R&D cost | Small piece of large pie<br>Less prestige<br>Can become very competitive | Minnetonka liquid soap<br>IBM personal computer<br>Panasonic VHS VCR<br>StressTabs vitamins<br>Colgate baking soda toothpaste<br>Healthy Choice frozen dinners<br>Arm & Hammer dryer sheets |
| Line extensions | Presold audience<br>Keeps brand fresh and new | Inferior product can dilute core brand | Healthy Choice soups<br>Compaq laptop computer<br>Haagen Daz frozen yogurt<br>Sara Lee fat-free cakes<br>Sony Walkman variations |
| New use | No new manufacturing costs<br>Incremental sales opportunity | | Arm & Hammer baking soda as refrigerator deodorizer<br>Jell-O Jigglers<br>Planters Good Measure nuts (for baking) |
| New for you | Existing market | Tendency to jump in without proper research | Thrive hair vitamins<br>Conair telephones<br>Citrus Hill orange juice |
| Next generation | Existing market<br>Keeps you ahead of competition<br>Makes competitive products seem old<br>Helps fend off price competition | Sell-in to retailers key<br>Consumers may resist frills | Computers (almost anyone's)<br>Citrus Hill orange juice with calcium |

A major success was created by the Lactaid Company. It markets an enzyme to help lactose-intolerant people digest milk and dairy products. After many years of groundwork, the product took off in a big way and generated big sales in the mass market when people started recognizing the problem and the Lactaid solution. The Lactaid people simply discovered a need—that was always there even if it wasn't recognized by the consumer—and filled it.

A different type of breakthrough product was the Wacky Wallwalker—a rubber kid's toy that was a mini-fad in the 1980s—which was developed by Ken Hakuta, marketer *cum* TV host. Hakuta is an example of an individual breaking all the rules and becoming rich. This is a rarity however. The majority of fads end up two for a dime at Joe's Pushcart Job Lot Stores—where Vegematics go to die. The Pet Rock is the patron saint of crazy ideas that somehow worked and, along with the Frisbee, has inspired multitudes of faddists-to-be.

Research and development departments tend to live for breakthrough products. But that's not where the *quickest* and *surest* financial returns are. Unfortunately R&D departments can get caught up in their own technology and are often out of touch with the real world of consumers or the harsh money restraints of business. Try telling an engineer that even though her or his new dispenser is a masterpiece of technological eloquence and an exquisite melding of rare materials, you have no product that would benefit from it.

Breakthrough new products are the hardest to manage. Those who can handle the consistent pressures are those who are willing to risk it all in the hope of getting it all. These are the kind of products and maverick entrepreneurs we read about in *Fortune* magazine.

*A new product can be an adaptation of an existing product.* This is where the bulk of new products are. This category offers the new-product developer the best chance of success. Most successful new products are adaptations of existing products that have already blazed themselves a consumer trail. The difference between a breakthrough product and an adaptive one is often one of degree. Minnetonka's Liquid Soap (soap in a container instead of a bar) and Lederle Lab's StressTabs (a vitamin positioned for people with stressful lives) were examples of breakthrough products that were simply adding new twists to existing categories.

Here is a money-saving marketing tip: Even a bit player or small marketing department can have an advantage over the big guns in adapting a product because the smaller player can react faster. One strategy is to find a category that is dominated by two or three companies and outflank them in areas they're missing. Unless your category grows enormously, the giants will usually ignore you because it's simply not worth their while to attack you.

When a large company does jump into a category and spends huge amounts, it is often creating awareness and interest for the category as a whole. Your piece of the pie may be relatively small on a share-of-market basis, but your actual sales may be more than substantial because you're sharing in a bigger pie. Lactaid has at least three competitors that it didn't have when the company was struggling, but these competitors are increasing consumer awareness for the entire category. Schick Razors has been following Gillette's new-product introductions for years. This allows them to save the enormous costs of advertising and R&D.

When you adapt another company's products though, you are usually relegated, like Schick, to the also-ran status in the category. That's not necessarily bad if you're interested in the financial and business rewards. The risk element is down too, since you are entering prewarmed market waters.

An adaptation can also be a *line extension* of your own product. Leveraging an existing trademark—the brand's ultimate consumer net worth—can be a quick and efficient strategy for entering a market because you don't have to spend tons of money introducing the brand.

What is a line extension anyway? A line extension is like a movie sequel—a product that relies on its parent "key," or brand name, to build share. Movie sequels attempt to parlay the success of a brand name to create an almost-new product.

You only have to sell a sequel once. You have to sell the consumer the line extension every time out. And you have to get the retailer to stock it. With consumer goods, the ultimate question is "What's left of the brand image when the coupons run out?" Marketers and R&D departments run the risk of playing havoc with their brands and their supporting retailers when they play fast and loose with the brand that "brought" them to the party. It's a paradox that the same people who moan about the lack of brand loyalty and cannibalization keep groping after new, and often inferior, line extensions. An example of a brand that's been messed up by line extensions is Nescafe. With line extensions such as Classic, Brava, and Mountain Blend coffees, who knows what the name Nescafe stands for anymore?

Leveraging an existing trademark can be a quick and efficient strategy for entering a market, saving gobs of money that would be spent playing new-product roulette—introducing and building awareness for a completely new brand. Line extensions can also defend store turf against the unwelcome intrusion of competing products.

Line extensions should vitalize the brand—not milk the brand—by reinforcing and building on brand qualities when the product enters the home. The key is to determine the equities and emotional properties of your brand and product and to ensure that the line extensions stay focussed and actually improve on the brand image.

*A new product can be a new use or a new market for an existing product.* This may sound like fudging on our definition of a new product, but it really isn't. Few of us would consider Jell-O a new product, but the Jell-O brand manager recently created a promotion called Jigglers which sold Jell-O to a new audience of kids that had passed it by.

Sales for a new use are almost always incremental. It may even be more propitious to dust off and revitalize that "golden oldie" than to develop a new product from scratch. We tend to get bored with and underrate the equity of our own existing products that are taking up space on the shelves long before the consumer does. Chapter 10 offers a complete program for identifying and revitalizing golden oldies.

*A new product can be a product that's new to your business...or a new business.* Arm & Hammer has made a living off this. By putting its name on various household products, it has created a business of well over three hundred million dollars. Arm & Hammer is constantly redefining its product line and now sells laundry detergents, dryer sheets, and various household deodorants. None of this was planned by Church & Dwight, Arm & Hammer's managing corporation, when the firm started selling a low-priced commodity—baking soda—over a hundred years ago.

Sometimes you have to offer a new product as a defensive measure. Gillette had to introduce their own stainless steel razor blades to resist the onslaught of other razor blade companies like Wilkinson and Personna.

The computer industry is always manic with new products because competition is constantly forcing a "new product or die" approach to the marketplace.

Your ego may be a driving force as you try to enter a category that you know little about, but a huge ego usually works to the detriment of the new-product developer or program. Do you salivate as you watch other companies capture market shares and big bucks and long for a piece of the action? Shulton was caught up in this exact situation several years ago. It had watched while Minnetonka imported a new hair-vitamin preparation called Foltene. A no-brainer, thought Shulton management, as it introduced a similar product called Thrive. "If they can do it, so can we," thought management. The Shulton product died a mercifully quick death. Shulton was never able to establish, in the male consumer's mind, exactly what the product actually did. Mighty Procter and Gamble (P&G) fell into the same trap when it watched the mighty profits made by orange juice and soda companies without realizing the nuances of the consumer market and distribution chain. Neither of its products (Citrus Hill orange juice and Hires root beer) have been big hits. P&G eventually had to take its losses and sold the soft drink business.

*A new product can be a next-generation product.* New-product development is a Darwinian struggle. You should keep moving and changing and improving, lest your market share be gobbled up by someone bigger, leaner, stronger, or more agile. Believe it or not, you should be trying to improve your products and work on new ones even before the core product is released into the stores. If you don't, your competitors will.

But no matter how you categorize new products, they represent major opportunities to today's aware marketer. There are always product opportunities where the zeitgeist of the time creates special needs. As this is being written, fat-free ice creams (an oxymoron if there ever was one) and frozen yogurts are the rage. So are fitness clubs and fitness machines. Consumers have been bombarded about the dangers of fat for years. Finally, they're getting the message. Manufacturers are adapting new technologies and adopting (there are those words again) new buzzwords to fulfill this relatively new consumer perceived need. These companies are, correctly, reacting to an evolving—and aging—marketplace.

New-product development doesn't take place in a vacuum. The world's seemingly endless display of consumer products has not grown by giant leaps and bounds but through the slow buildup of minor advances that created small joys or solved small problems. These products also took creative marketing and insightful thinking, as in the marketing of Life Savers.

**Slice of Life**

Nobody really set out to invent Life Savers candy. It was an afterthought by a candy maker who was trying to sell something besides perishable chocolate to fill the lag in sales during the hot summer months. The new candy sold poorly. The breakthrough came when an advertising salesman came along and bought the failing hard candy business for the proverbial song. After trying and failing with different strategies, he wrapped the product in foil to preserve freshness and persuaded cigar and candy vendors to place it near the cash register, where consumers would pick up a roll instead of taking a nickel in change. The product quickly caught on, and the humble round candy spawned the myriad of new impulse products we see crowding the cash register today.

## Why Some Products Succeed But Many More Don't

Why do most new products fail? It's not that they're bad ideas, many are quite good, and R&D technologies are getting better and better. The products fail because they don't solve an emotional or physical need and haven't staked out a footprint on the shelves or in the consumer's life. They haven't created the needed emotional link with consumers. *They are random solutions searching for problems to solve.*

Most products fail because companies try to sell people what the companies want to *sell* rather than what consumers want to buy. A prime example is the U.S. car makers who are continually crying that the Japanese won't buy their new products. But guys, the Japanese have their steering wheels on the right side and you won't put them there for the Japanese market!

When was the last time you talked to consumers and asked them about their needs? They're coming at new products from a totally different angle than you are. New-products people talk about features. Consumers talk about benefits. These are two different concepts. Consumers buy benefits, not features.

## The Eleven Most Common Excuses for Doing It Wrong

Among the alibis I hear often are:

1. "But my business is different."
2. "We have too many government regulations to deal with."
3. "We sell only to highly specialized industries."
4. "We don't have the time or money for market research."
5. "Engineering just came up with this wonderful idea."
6. "Marketing just came up with this wonderful idea."
7. "There are no new ideas."
8. "We tried that five years ago."
9. "We never tried that before."
10. "We don't do it that way here."
11. "I know what works."

All business people swear that their business is different from any other business. This is simply not so.

## The Path of Least Consumer Resistance

No matter what your business is, or what you want it to be, it depends on selling something to someone else. The most efficient way to do this is to take the path of least consumer resistance—to find a need and fill it.

An estimated 10,000 new products were introduced last year. If you lined them up, end to end, you'd have, well, you'd have an incredible waste of space. You'd also have an idea of the kind of competition that's out there and why you need a consumer edge.

The latest industry figures reveal that, at most, only about 1500 of those products that were introduced are still around; 8500 bit the dust. Surprisingly the failure rate is not the fault of the much ballyhooed word that's used as a crutch—the devil *undercapitalization.* Of course, having almost adequate funds (you never really have enough) is important, but it can be just as easy to blow a $10,000,000 budget as a $10,000 stake. The process just takes a bit longer.

## Going Down the Wrong Path with Statistics

People come up to me excited about an idea through the sheer power of numbers. Typical of this is a business plan for a new deodorant or snack food that has to capture only 1 percent of a market to survive. That's right, the marketing whiz shouts, "If only 1 out of every 100 people buy our product once a week we'll have a $25 million business!" Trouble is, it doesn't work that way, even though it does look good on the premarket report or business plan. It doesn't work that way because your competitors would probably be pitching that same product to the same consumers. The quickest and best returns on your new-product investment come from creating an idea for a highly targeted niche market and getting the product to the consumer faster and better than your competition does.

Running rings around your competition means working smarter than your competition, not necessarily outspending them. New-product development is a combination of brains and material. The more brains you use, the less material you need.

- Smarter means solving a new consumer need in a way that nobody has before.
- Smarter means not trying to outguess consumers but working with them to find out their needs.
- Smarter means being personally involved with all consumer and market research and not being impressed by the secondhand nonsense of 500-page reports.
- Smarter means research, research, and more research.
- Smarter means evolving and learning. Smarter means continuous auditioning of your product until you're sure you have a winner, and not taking short cuts.

- Smarter means knowing that consumers are interested in your product only as it pertains to them.
- Smarter means having everyone who is part of the new-product team—even your crack engineers and R&D people—react with consumers.
- Smarter means not allowing preconceived notions to color your judgment.

The successful new-product developer manages evolution and change, planning for a chaotic environment. The phrase "What can happen now?" is a major phrase of the new-product-development person's lexicon.

The successful new-product developer actually encourages serendipity, those happy and surprise accidents that can lead to a successful new product or strategy when you keep a wide open mind. Inelastic approaches to product development rarely work, since the dynamics of the marketplace and even the mindset of the consumer are constantly changing.

Products live and die by how the consumer perceives them. To consumers, the *perception is the reality, even if it's wrong.*

It's funny but some of the most experienced marketers complain that customers don't know about or buy the best product or don't care about how hard the company worked to keep the price down.

Why should they?

Here are some other things the consumer doesn't care about:

The cleverness of your R&D department.

Your marketing goals.

What it costs you to make the product.

Whether you make money.

Whether you stay in business (usually).

How dramatically advanced your product is.

Here's a test. Ask a consumer about the last new product tried (at New Products Workshop we do this all the time). The consumer will almost always come back with something you might consider mundane, inaccurate, and, to you, as a marketer, even foolish. The consumer might say a new flavor soup, a new kind of snack food. Maybe even Jigglers from Jell-O. To the consumer, these are new, exciting, and different.

There is no interest like self-interest, and consumers will fool you every time.

**Pop Quiz**

The goal of your new-product development program is to maintain an optimum balance of cost and quality while utilizing your corporate systems and technologies to their fullest extent; to develop leading-edge engineering technologies and stretch your engineering resources to their limits. True or false?

*False.* The goal is to make a product consumers want at a price they can afford, in the simplest way possible—so that you can make money.

A key and almost universal mistake that small entrepreneurs make is to get an idea and treat it like it was the Holy Grail. Entrepreneurs spend their life's savings on a whim and a prayer trying to market their products because they are convinced the world is going to stand in line for them. They back it when all the evidence points against it. One client kept asking people whether they liked or disliked his product. When they said it was terrible, he said they weren't his target audience. When one in a hundred said it was okay, he would point his finger and shout, "SEE, I TOLD YOU—All I need is one in a hundred." He didn't get it.

Or larger companies get hung up in the marketing plan. They're dazzled by the bright lights of their own overhead projector and the momentum of papers shuffling back and forth. They quickly find out that no one gives a damn about the cleverness of their engineering or R&D department.

To summarize our new-product development process, like the old airline commercial said—getting there is half the fun. To many entrepreneurs, getting there is all the fun. Here's a quick summary of basic premises:

- Our knowledge and ideation will start from ground zero. No preconceptions, no relying on past research. Traditional research tells what happened in the past—we want to know how to anticipate current and future needs.
- We work in a real-world environment, using graphic color concepts of hypothetical products or positionings to function as "fuel" for the expression of need satisfaction by consumers. We challenge consumers to buy.
- We're interested in underlying behavior patterns of consumers—their values, attitudes, and lifestyles.
- We will adapt and evolve our concepts and products as we learn more about what drives the consumer and the market.

- Ideation never stops. We will continue to evolve our products until we arrive at the one that will achieve our goals and satisfies a consumer need.

New-product development is an action arena where you constantly stretch the limits of your marketing instinct and where you must leave your ego waiting in the car.

Someone asked an old entertainer—a 50-year show business veteran—the secret of his success: His basic act had never changed—audiences still paid to see him and to laugh at jokes they had probably heard many times before.

"Once you find out what your audience wants, you give it to 'em the way they want it. Tell 'em what they want to hear. Show 'em what they want to see. And sell it with a smile."

That's also our secret to new product development success: Find out what the consumers want. Find out the way they want it. Sell it to them that way.

## Summary

1. Just as there's always room for Jell-O, there's always room for new products when you identify and fulfill a need. Consumer needs are constantly evolving as new products are added to the U.S. scene.
2. Consumers buy benefits, not products or features. A lasting key to success is to find a need and fill it. Make or sell consumers something they want to buy, not what you want to sell them.
3. So-called breakthrough products are rarely successes. The surest chance of success is to sell what's selling...to adapt an already successful product and to build something special into it.

## Questions, Answers, and Additional Insights

*How important are new products, really?*

In a study of CEOs of major food companies by Edward Ogiba that appeared in *Food & Beverage Marketing,* a respected food industry trade journal, 61 percent said they expected new products to contribute 30 percent of sales in the following five years. A rule of thumb is that to handle competitive pressures, a medium-sized company should expect new products to generate at least 25 percent of sales over the following five-year period.

*Which are the most active industries in new product development?*
According to the same study, the most innovative industries (based on new product introductions) are:

Food and beverage: 45 percent

Communication/transportation services: 15 percent

Soft goods: 13 percent

Durable goods: 11 percent

Health and beauty aids: 7 percent

Household goods: 5 percent

Financial services: 3 percent

Other: 1 percent

*With all we have learned about new-product development, why has the failure rate not changed drastically?*
Despite allegedly improved marketing practices, the failure rate of new products has remained steady over the past 20 years. The lack of useful and current research is King Culprit. Other reasons include lack of strategic direction (poor research again), lack of management and R&D involvement, and the necessity for short payback periods.

*What does it take to win?*
Ogiba quotes Nabisco's president and CEO in *Food & Beverage Marketing:* "The successful companies will be those that maintain clear strategic direction and management commitment, while staying in touch with the needs of consumers and the changing external environment." That's a fancy way of saying adapt and adopt and give the consumer what the consumer wants.

*I've always worked for someone else, and I have a new idea that I know would be great. How do I get started?*
First, make sure that other people share your enthusiasm and draw up a business plan. The library will have tons of books that will give you all sorts of plans. Then follow the process spelled out in the following chapters. Spend a little on research before you commit the big money.

*My company gives lip service to new-product development, but everything I come up with is either shot down or starts slow and management quickly pulls the plug. What do I do?*

Unfortunately, most large companies are like that. Publicly, for the stockholders and media ears, companies will take an aggressive stance when it comes to new-product development. Privately, many admit the new-product area is a training ground for marketing juniors fresh out of MBA school.

*I've just opened a new wine and spirits store. I've stocked it with wines that I know are good, but my customers keep buying cheap jug wines. What do I do?* Stock plenty of cheap jug wines for your accountant to pay bills. If you have extra money, you can carry the extra bottles for the occasional buyer and your ego. Sell what's selling.

# 2
# The Idea as God

*Chapter preview:*

- ***Where to find the next big idea (how to generate a successful idea search)***
- ***Ideas as the seed of your new product***
- ***Radical hypothezation***
- ***How to read your own mind for the big idea***
- ***Setting the stage for Eureka***
- ***Selecting your key people***
- ***One-sentence solutions to life's problems***
- ***The one word that can stop an idea in its tracks***
- ***Scamper—the "compleat" brainstormer***

What is so big it can change the earth? Yet so small, nobody has ever seen one....So powerful, it can move people past the barriers of our solar system...(where no one has ever gone before), yet so volatile it will vaporize in the time it takes to read this sentence. So widespread that everyone has hundreds a day....So easy to kill, all it takes is a two-letter word....

It's an *idea.* Extol the paradox of the great idea! It is worth nothing but it is worth everything. Raw ideas to the new-product development person are like pencil sketches to an oil painter—marks to be worked with, adapted, and manipulated.

Most of the people who call my office ask for advice but really want two other things—agreement with and encouragement for their ideas. The first one I rarely give, and the latter I always provide absolutely free.

### Pop Quiz

Which of the following ideas would you have backed?

1. You press a button on the 4-inch plastic cube and you hear a whirring sound. Slowly and steadily a miniature skeleton

of a hand crawls forth from the ebony cube. It touches the same button on the cube that you did. The whirring stops, the hand darts back into the cube. That's it.

2. Your coworker mixes up a vat of glue that fails to adhere properly. Instead of throwing it out, he brushes it on the back of small pieces of paper and uses them to mark his place in his bible. Then he tries to sell it to management.
3. A major consumer electronics company has an idea for a unique electronics player that shows theatrical films on home TV. The company signs a contract with major studios to ensure that this invention would be stocked with major releases.
4. A small company has created new technology and patented machinery to create an ice cream cone from pretzel dough. The baker, a small entrepreneurial type, puts salt on the cone because he thinks people will learn to like salt with ice cream.

The successes were numbers 1 and 2. The black box sold for about $10 and had an enormously long sales life. The substandard glue, of course, became the key component of 3M's ubiquitous Post-it-Notes.

The failure was—surprise—number 3. RCA invested $400 million in its ill-fated video disk player, which became the most expensive anchor in the world.

The pretzel cone can go either way.

## The Quest for the Big Idea

We probably all can't hit a grand slam home run in the bottom of the ninth in front of 50,000 people. We probably won't win an Oscar or even strike oil while cleaning out our septic system. But we can all come up with the big idea at least once in our lives if we have the wherewithal and the discipline to make it happen.

A successful idea search can bring you closer to your goals. An idea search can help you generate better ideas.

### The Product Idea Is the Seed of What's to Come

The successful new-product search in a product development program begins not with a product idea but with a search for the solution to an underlying consumer need that you can fill. The goal of an idea search is to furnish the raw material for a product that will make the earth move for someone (and, of course, to make money for your company).

The successful idea search explores all ends of the creative spectrum, stretching the boundaries of what can be done. It also ignores technological limits. It's amazing how technology will fall into place when you find a consumer need to solve. The Voyager rocket that took photos of Uranus in 1988 was directed by software that wasn't even invented in the 1970s, when the rocket was launched. Scientists figured they would come up with the solution when they had to. They did. Find the need first, and if there's money to be made, you're sure to figure out how to do it. Fred Smith of Federal Express fame built his company on the simple concept of next-day delivery—first he had the concept, and then he figured out how to get it done. This is a 360-degree turnaround from the usual "let's button-up everything and then figure out why people would want it." To put it even more simply, *find the what and the why, and you'll come up with the how later.*

Another reason to ignore technological limits (within reason, of course) is that a technically unworkable idea can lead to one that is doable. As most writers know, it's more efficient to edit out an idea than have to scour your brain for a new one. To delete, all it takes is an eraser or blue pen (or the handy escape button on my computer).

This might seem like we're going to build a product backward. But are we? If we were going to build a building, we would first start with a blueprint, speculating on the future inhabitants and how they would use the structure. Then we would make changes to our paper blueprint when we found out what was really important to the inhabitants. This would be done way before we placed the first brick. It's pretty expensive to make changes to a house that's already built.

We're going to build our new product the same way. We're going to find out what the consumer's needs and wants are before we commit the big bucks. Instead of trying to sell a product to the consumer, like most companies and inventors mistakenly do (did anyone mention the 85 percent failure rate?), we're going to find the perceived emotional or physical consumer need first and then fill this need.

If you already have the product, fear not—we're going to find the consumer hook to make sure it sells or make minor changes to the product to make sure we're on the money.

## Radical Hypothezation

*Radical hypothezation* is coming up with marketing theories that explore all polarities of the new-product spectrum. Radical hypothezation is the casting of a big idea net. There are many, many ways to solve a problem or create a need. The net captures the ideas so they can be inspected for viability and potential. These ideas are then cast out as lures to attract even bigger and better ideas, just as a large fish will often eat, and be nourished by, the smaller fish.

For instance, let's go back a few eons and suppose video stores hadn't been invented and a person wanted to open one up. Most people would limit their thinking to a nice little store in a mall—pretty decor, wall-to-wall displays, perhaps a fake fern or two, a major bank loan to pay off. That's conventional thinking. The traffic potential is limited to your neighborhood population, your finances, and the competition that's bound to spring up.

Let's look at some options that might be considered if we let our mind expand on the opportunity—if we hypothesize to all ends of the spectrum.

A medium-sized store in a mall

A series of boutique shops in little delis. You give the owners the videos free in return for space and share in the profits

Video kiosks in supermarkets and department stores

Videos by mail

A video megastore

How about sending tapes over phone lines and capturing them with a home computer? Now I know this one isn't technically feasible for the home user—yet—but it's better to have an idea, consider it, and throw it out than to not have it at all. All the above video store ideas, in fact, except for the last have proven to be a window of opportunity for one marketer or another.

To decide which one would be the best, all ideas first have to be caught in the net and displayed so they can be evaluated and acted upon. That's what radical hypothezation does. Radical hypothezation is simply a concrete extension of the thought process. Radical hypothezation is the opposite of tunnel vision.

The mission of radical hypothezation is to develop alternatives to solving consumer needs—to hypothesize consumer wants and to create hypothetical products to fulfill these needs. When we develop the new product our way, we will also be learning the purchase triggers that will make the product a success so you don't have any expensive false starts.

This method has also been proven for repositioning existing products—even those that failed—because when you are repositioning a product you are essentially creating a new product in the consumer's mind.

## How to Read Your Own Mind for the Big Idea

I often think of getting out of my business. In fact, I complain about the hassles so vigorously that one day one of my staffers silk-screened a plaque for my office that perfectly echoed my thinking. It says, "I gotta get out of this business...get me a little fruit stand."

I mentioned this to a client one day, an entrepreneurial type, and he laughed.

"You know what...once you get that fruit stand, you'll drive yourself crazy with new ideas about what kind of fruit to sell. Then you'll try to get bigger and better fruit. Then you'll try to grow the fruit yourself or invent new fruit. Then you'll dream about a string of fruit stands. You'll keep coming up with new ideas and you'll never be satisfied...because that's what you do."

He's right. For most entrepreneurial types, the ideas never stop coming. In fact, for entrepreneurial types, the money that can be made takes second billing to creating the product. It's the job of the new-product manager to capture and channel these ideas.

An idea can come at any moment. It doesn't matter what age you are or what education level you've achieved as long as you're secure enough (crazy enough?) to buck the "accepted wisdom" or "common knowledge" of the times. It was a 58-year-old Italian taxi driver with a fourth-grade education who created Tropicana fresh-squeezed orange juice because he saw a need. Apparently he didn't learn enough in grade school to know you can't ship fresh orange juice any kind of distance. Seagram's recently purchased Tropicana for a huge sum of money, and MBAs are still swearing that you shouldn't ship fresh-squeezed orange juice.

You also have to know when to back off a bad idea. This same inventor spent the rest of his life trying to perfect and sell the optimal fig.

Creativity is not only about writing poetry, composing sonatas, or painting masterpieces. These are only the store-bought products of creativity. Creativity in new-product development is about breaking the bounds of patterned thought to uncover a consumer need and solve the problem in a new way—eliminating the preconceived notion of what can and cannot be done. The preconceived notion is the major enemy to most new-product programs. Take these examples:

"Everything that can be invented, has been invented." Charles H. Duell, director of U.S. Patent Office, 1899.

"Who the hell wants to hear actors talk?" Harry M. Warner, Warner Brothers Pictures, 1927.

"Heavier-than-air flying machines are impossible." Lord Kelvin, President, Royal Society, 1895.

Creativity is prey for the preconceived notion and the naysayers. We have taught ourselves not to think. We have applied the tightest censorship to our own minds. Childhood creativity is not outgrown. It is slain by the rapiers of ridicule and disapproval. Part of the reason for the lack of creativity of many MBAs (admittedly this is a somewhat broad generalization) is because, in business school, students are instructed to follow patterns and existing ways of doing things:

"Do it this way."

"Why?"

"Because this is the way it's always been done."

"Oh."

Literally everyone has ideas throughout the day. I call it "mind chatter." It is the sound you make when you talk to yourself. The problem is that few people know how to channel these extraordinary electric impulses or discern the good chatter from the destructive kind. An idea by itself is neither inherently good nor inherently bad until we instill the idea with consumer value. Serendipity can be a major source of ideas, because it can provide you with unexpected inspiration. Ivory soap was created by accident when a production worker accidentally pumped a bar of soap too full of air. Creative marketers implied that the bar actually floated because it was so pure—an example of taking advantage of serendipity.

Serendipity always occurs—and should be allowed to occur—in the new-product process. If it doesn't, you're too rigid in your thinking or simply not working hard enough.

## Requisites for the Innovator

You, as the originator of the new-product idea, are in a semi-weird position. As the product's champion, you must think your product is the best the world has ever seen. And when you sell it to people—managers, investors, etc.—you must treat it as if it were the third coming of Elvis. Enthusiasm is truly contagious.

But you must be an editor too. And a bit of a realist. Because absolutely no one is going to be as excited about your ideas as you are.

You must be willing to make changes as you go along or to drop a bad idea. That's not as easy as it sounds. When you've invested all that energy, money, and time in an idea, not to mention staring at the ceiling at 4:00 a.m. and fantasizing about a new Porsche in the driveway (it'll look silly outside an apartment), you're going to find it hard to stop all that momentum. It can be especially difficult to drop or change an idea when it's the only one you have, and everything depends on that one idea.

But, when you develop a quantity of ads and premises, however, instead of just one or two, and if the first ones don't work out, you can simply move on to a better one.

### Separating the Good from the Bad—One-Sentence Solutions to Life's Problems

Every new product should start with an idea and a one-word question—why? Why would anyone want this product? How long would it take you to explain the product benefits to your customer? If you can't explain your reason to the customer in one sentence—or less—then you really don't have a product. Think it's tough selling a product in a sentence? The Ten Commandments were written on two plaques.

Feig's Law is: the strength of an idea is inverse to the number of footnotes and attributes needed to sell the idea. Some marketing plans for even the simplest products look like they were written by graduates of the school for obfuscation and redundancy.

### How to Set the Stage for Eureka

Occasionally I'm asked where I come up with my ideas (the heart of my business). I tell people I ask my carpenter the same thing. Probably unwittingly, we've trained our minds until creative thinking has become a habit. You can do it too. It's startlingly simple. Three little words:

Immerse

Forget

Stimulate

The creative mind has to be constantly fed and nourished with inspiration. That's why the offices and homes of "creative" types tend to be monuments to disorganization. Disorganization and chaos seem to be how, perhaps unconsciously, the creative mind immerses itself in data and draws connections to seemingly random bits of information. Surprisingly, applied creativity relies less on the unrestricted explosions of ideas than on forming patterns between seemingly unrelated pieces of information.

Get all the information you can on a subject. *Immerse* yourself. Read. Think. Talk to people who know more than you do. Magazine editors are great sources of information and inspiration. Call the editors of magazines that deal in your prospective product category. You'll be amazed how willing they'll be to talk. While talking to an editor about new soft drinks, he introduced me to a person who collects ginger ales. Really. This person had collected cans, ads, and actual samples of over a thousand ginger ales dating back a hundred years. God knows why. My client, who was looking for new brand and flavor opportunities, was thrilled.

Keep your eyes and ears open until your mind is literally bursting with knowledge. Treat your mind like it's a sponge. Absorb everything. Go to libraries, watch TV, talk to consumers, examine absolutely everything that's slightly related to the problem or subject without worrying if it really makes sense. That's what I recently did while working on a project for Mitsubishi conveyors. I knew nothing going in, but because I was unbridled by preconceived notions about what would and wouldn't work, I was able to come up with information that everyone else—even Mitsubishi—had missed. That's what successful new product development is about—finding something that everyone else missed.

After you've immersed yourself, then *forget* everything. Wring out your mind. Play racquetball. Knit. Go shopping. Make love. In some unexplained way your mind is going to search—and find—a pattern amid this chaos. And really, what is chaos but an unperceived pattern?

Then *stimulate* your mind with the problem. This is the complicated part, because you won't know where or how the answer will come about. This can get touchy if you decided to make love and the answer pops up at a key moment.

Want proof? Think of doing a crossword puzzle. You're stumped on a word. You try and try. You beat your head against the wallboard. Still the word won't appear. So you forget it. You go to the bathroom, or go to sleep, or take a walk, or grab a sandwich. Then, you pick up the puzzle, and the answer magically pops into your head.

Why? Unless you cheated and went to the dictionary, you obviously weren't any smarter than you were when you started the puzzle only a few hours before. The answer was in your brain all the time—on hold. All the time it was waiting to release itself. I'm not going to pretend I know why this happens, but it does—I've built my career on this phenomenon.

*Never be without the following essential high-tech tool:* How many times have you said "I had a great idea but I forgot it." Always carry a pen or pencil. Put one by the bed or even in the bathroom. This may sound silly, basic, condescending, or all three, but it is essential to be well-armed at all times. Ideas are not 9-to-5 creatures. They can and will burst forth at any time. My friends who run businesses all talk about scribbling ideas in the middle of the freeway. (Kids, don't try this at home or in Dad's car.) Some people prefer mini-tape recorders, especially the voice-activated kind, but I've found that forcing your fingers to react to your mind reinforces the idea and spurs the imagination. Whichever system you prefer, remember an idea is a fragment of thought that you can lose in less than an instant. Don't blow a million-dollar idea for lack of a nineteen-cent pen.

*The supermarket and mall as laboratory.* To the dedicated new-products specialist, supermarkets, stores, and malls are more than places to buy things. They are labs of consumer needs and motivations. You can watch products get old, wither, and die and be replaced by newer, improved models.

Any product that crosses your path can be an inspiration for a new product if you let it. Later you'll get ideas on how you can turn the most mundane of aisles and products into veritable gardens of inspiration.

*Trade shows, book stores, and more as laboratory.* Fill your head with minutiae no matter where you are. It doesn't even have to be a category you're working on. A computer trade show might lend itself to a new product for a car. Force one technology into another and see what you can build in your mind. An in-dash microwave oven in a car for heating "portable car foods" might be an idea waiting to be discovered (please send royalty checks in care of this publisher).

*Your company archives or old magazines as laboratory.* Just because your predecessor came up with the idea doesn't mean it's bad. Just because an idea didn't work before doesn't mean it can't work now. Put a new twist on it. Several years ago we created an American cheese product called Deli Singles for a northeast cheese maker. They thanked us for the job and put the work away in the desk. A year later I found the product in my local A&P. A new brand manager had come in, found the work in his files, ran with the idea, and became an instant hero—for it helped turn the declining market share around.

Review your company's history for products that didn't work before but might work now. Don't give up on marginal products too soon. Every R&D department has scads of well-thought-through ideas in their library that were abandoned for reasons unknown. Perhaps lack of a sponsor, the time just wasn't right, the politics were wrong, or nobody thought of the little consumer twist that was necessary to make it a big success. The consumer doesn't care where your idea comes from as long as it solves a need. Old magazines can also serve as a spark for new ideas that you can adapt, adopt, and bring up to date.

## Your New-Product Task Force: Select It Early

Developing a new product for a large or medium-sized company is always a compromise between job functions and departments. It's vital to bring together the key disciplines (i.e., R&D, engineering, operations, even possible vendors) at the earliest possible time. Ideas and input are needed from the beginning and throughout the project. Talented people know that ideas rarely occur between 9:00 and 5:00. When you enlist your team early on, the members tend to give your product discretionary "thought time." This also tends to preempt defensive turf battles and insecurities which spring up among latecomers to the project. Foster a vested interest in the project as a whole, rather than its parts, among the selected individuals. Of course, you don't want a compromise product, a product built by committee. This kind of product benefits no one and usually succeeds in eliciting yawns instead of sales from the consumer.

It is your goal to provide a conduit for new ideas—to develop and concentrate energies within departmental structures, gently spurring the process onward.

## Create a Tight Deadline

Choose a deadline, even if it's artificial and unrealistic, then keep it. Don't wait for the muse: There's no such thing. In the new-products business you have to force time and make things happen. If you don't, your competitor surely will. Every good creative person can come in under a deadline whether it's in a month or the next day. Most artists and copywriters won't pick up a pen or touch a typewriter until the deadline is on top of them. In the new-product business, patience is bad. Impatience is good.

The difference between a strong idea search and a weak one is a matter of intensity. When I was approached to do this book, I set an impossible deadline—I wanted the adrenaline rush to keep me interested. Little did I know my unconscionable editor would hold me to it. A project will always expand to fit the time allotted, but the interest and enthusiasm level will taper off greatly the longer it drags on.

Here's a neat management trick: Give people an idea of the project even before the project is definitely set. Whether they want to or not, most people will unconsciously work through the assignment in their mind—like a puzzle. They'll be fully prepared when the project commences.

## About Brainstorming Companies—They're Fun But Extremely Limited and Expensive

The Synectics approach is an elaborate development of brainstorming, but in my opinion, it's more flash and mirrors than effectiveness. In traditional Synectics (a trade name), a project team is created of a half dozen of your people with different talents and backgrounds. They meet, usually off site for a couple of days, as a group leader takes them through various creative activities, not totally unlike what you did in third grade. They make use of free association, metaphors, role playing, living out problems, and analogies. The analogies used are personal, direct, symbolic, and fantastic.

One Synectics off-shoot supposedly releases your inner child by having you play and doodle in clay or Play-Doh. It's great fun if you're running short on ashtrays and have a kiln handy. And they make great Christmas gifts.

The major problem—the fatal flaw—is the process includes little or no editing, which is as vital to the new product process as it is to a movie. The typical product is a thousand-page report with about two hundred one-liners that collects dust on someone's desk.

A major financial company hired a group to help them brainstorm ideas. They ended up with over two hundred ideas with no focus, no reason for being, because there was no editing process. The pages were filled with things like, "I would like a loan I never have to pay back." "I'd like a pill that turns into money." The firm had paid over $200,000 for this study. It then hired us to make sense of this drivel and turn it into a viable consumer-driven product.

The other fatal flaw is that thinking stops after the report is generated. All ideation sessions and most new-product development programs assume that the winning idea is going to come out of the initial batch—sort of like a funnel. (See Fig. 2-1*a*.)

The idea session is only the very first thinking process. New ideas must constantly be generated as we learn more about our market and we narrow out the learning curve with consumer insights. Almost never does the preliminary ideation contain the full answer. Perhaps only minor tinkering and changes are necessary. Perhaps the manager will need to change his or her total expectations of the project.

If you charted it out, it would look like a two-humped camel as you continually generate new ideas and learn more about your market and how your product will fit in. (See Fig. 2-1*b*.)

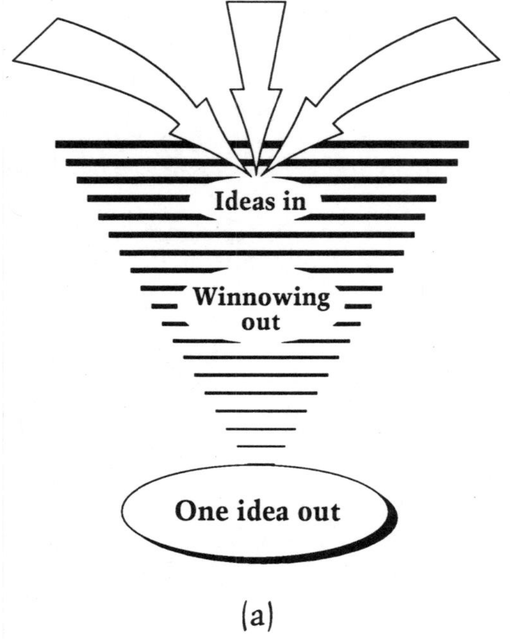


(a)

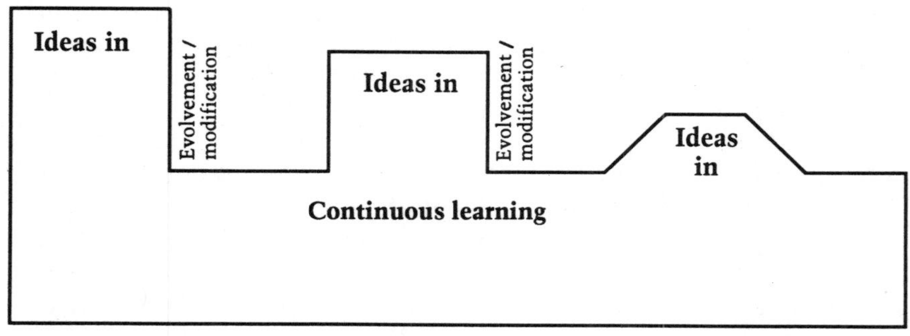


(b)

**Figure 2-1.** Why assume the best idea is in the original batch? It almost never is! (*a*) Traditional ideation—limited and flawed. (*b*) NPW ideation—continuous and evolutionary.

## How to "Scamper" to a Successful Opportunity

The brain can do mystical magical things when we let it. The following is adapted from a wonderful little idea-generating system called Scamper by Robert Eberle. It's one of my favorite tools. It provides major sparks to creativity and is a key stimulus of my informal ideation sessions. (*Ideation* is the MBA word for brainstorming and radical hypothezation.)

The first letter of each category reading down spells *Scamper.* These are new ways of thinking about your product. Use this chart on your next supermarket lab or mall expedition, and let your mind play.

Substitute, Simplify
Change, Combine
Adapt, Adopt
Magnify, Minify
Modify, Multiply
Package, Purloin
Elevate, Eliminate
Reverse, Rearrange

1. *Substitute.* Substitute a better way for a consumer to do something, or replace an element that will be perceived as unique for your product. For instance, substitute fructose for refined sugar and create a product with a more wholesome image. Right now, marketers across America are frantically looking for ways to substitute fat-free analogs into our diet in place of the rich, cholesterol foods we love so dearly. Just recently, Pepsi-Cola substituted a clear color for their brown colored beverage in hopes of creating a new product.

2. *Simplify.* Make things simpler for a consumer's life. Lunch Bucket Meals by Armour, in a 7-ounce disposable, microwaveable container, made it easy to take meals to the office for microwaving.

3. *Change.* Change the formula of your product. Even if the recipe was handed down by your great grandmother, it wasn't written in stone. Change it, if necessary, to keep in tune with the consumer trends.

4. *Combine.* Combine two products or product benefits to make a stronger one. Procter and Gamble combined shampoo and conditioner to make Pert Plus, one of the leading hair care products of the nineties.

5. *Adapt.* Adapt a product or technology to move from one category to another. Today's ubiquitous fax is merely a computer adapted to one simple task—to send a printed message via telephone lines.

6. *Adopt.* Adopt products, uses, containers, packages, and technologies from one country or industry to another. There are many, many examples. American Cyanamid's Combat pesticide was adopted from their agricultural department's technology to make a pollution-free pest controller. Hair mousse was adopted from a European fad fashion trend.

7. *Magnify, minify.* Make your product larger or smaller. This is another idea that sounds so simple you tend to pass it buy. Nabisco created brand new opportunities when they downsized and upsized Oreo cookies and Ritz crackers. Create single-serve, family-sized, and travel configurations. Sony created a billion-dollar opportunity when it downsized its cassette stereo and called it a "Walkman."

8. *Modify.* Change your product to reflect new consumer wants and desires. Adult diapers and many women's sanitary products are merely modifications of disposable diapers.

9. *Multiply.* Six packs, twelve packs, and more can all help you change your product and increase sales.

10. *Package.* Repackage your product or service. I learned to write by reading the *New York Post*'s sports section. As an afternoon newspaper, the *Post* had no first-run news to offer. We all knew the sports scores from reading the morning papers or watching TV. Yet, the *New York Post* exists and even thrives (admittedly a subject of debate as this is being written) because the *Post* repackaged the news in a way that continued, and continues, to attract readers. Give your product a new wrap; make it more appealing to customers. Liquor companies always squeeze a few more sales during the holiday season by creating festive holiday packaging. By doing this they turn a product into a gift.

11. *Purloin.* Okay, steal. Now, I'm not talking about doing unethical or illegal things. But when a product is a success, it's fair game for everyone. There's nothing wrong with looking abroad for either a product or a product idea.

12. *Elevate.* Move your product to the head of a class with a more expensive price tag and elegant packaging. Examples abound. Did anyone say Grey Poupon?

13. *Eliminate.* Remove or eliminate a quality. Take away the sugar and fructose entirely from your soft drink and you have a lightly flavored seltzer. It's a half-billion-dollar business. An acquaintance who

bottled No-Cal sodas in New York said that was what was left when the government made them remove cyclamates. (We had actually recommended a similar product to a major soft drink company, but the firm passed on it when some MBA said he was told in marketing school not to ship water—the preconceived notion strikes again.)

14. *Reverse.* Do the opposite with your product. Explore all polarities of a product. Try a mild version of a sauce along with a hot one. Explore different taste and sensory sensations. A couple of years ago, a poorly shaven Don Johnson made the scruffy look chic; razors were promoted on their ability not to give a close shave.

15. *Rearrange.* Change the order and attributes of your product, layout, or scheme. Few people know that the familiar QWERTY typewriter keyboard (named after the first six letters on the second row) came about because typewriter manufacturers wanted to slow down the typing speeds of typists. Their machines simply could not keep up. That's why the *E* and the *T*, the most used letters, are on the top row of letters...so a typist would have to stretch.

## An Informal Brainstorming Session

Brainstorming (or ideating) is fun and simple. All brainstorming is based on the theory that it's hard to stop a runaway horse, which in this case is creativity.

The interesting thing is, like the runaway horse, creativity gives its most powerful kick when it's the most tired. The most cogent ideas are usually delivered when the mind relaxes and the coats are being donned.

Brainstorming simply involves getting a group of people together for a stated goal. There are a few simple processes and rules:

1. What you'll need:
   - Two hours in the morning and a conference room (round table preferred)
   - Easel and large pad (22 × 28 in)
   - Markers and masking tape
   - A copy of the Scamper chart
   - Two signs: "No Negativity" and "Everyone's Right"
   - The problem
   - Lots of coffee or tea

2. Invite anyone who has an interest in the project—all disciplines should be invited, including, if possible, your suppliers. Don't forget secretaries and the people who deliver the mail. Eight attendees is a comfortable number.
3. Provide a mission statement a day or so before the meeting.

A sample brainstorming session is shown in Fig. 2-2.

New Products Workshop, Inc.

212-370-0980

521 Fifth Avenue, 17th Floor
New York, NY 10175

SAMPLE BRAINSTORMING SESSION
(For format only; you'll be going into far more detail)

KEY STEP -- Introductions of people in the room.

KEY STEP -- STATE PURPOSE AND GOALS
"Thank you for coming. As you know from the memo I sent out, today we're going to come up with new prepared products that can be made with chicken that would be appealing to consumers.

We're going to pretend we're like God and that there are absolutely no limitations. If you were going to WISH for the perfect chicken for eating what would would it be like?"

(wait for response -- write all responses on the large pad)
sample response (Bill) "A chicken with five legs."

Why is that good?

(Bill) "...because I like dark meat."

"Good. Does anyone else feel that way?"

(Ellen) "I'd like one that's already cooked."

"Why?"

(Ellen) "Because I hate to cook and I want something fast for dinner."

"How should it be cooked?"

(Ellen) "With a lot of seasonings."

(Bill) "I don't like seasonings."

(Ernie) "Did anyone here ever try orange glazed chicken?"

(Ellen) "It's delicious. Could we make that in our test kitchens?"

"I don't know. Can we? Suppose we could. How many other kinds of chicken can we make?"

**Figure 2-2.** Sample brainstorming session.

At the meeting room, state and constantly restate the problem. Read aloud the different aspects of the Scamper chart. Emphasize the following:

1. No negativity. Try to build on every idea. No idea is impractical (yet). No telephone calls. No titles.
2. The ideas should be allowed to come in quantity with no judgments made.
3. Constantly state the problem, restate it, and look at it in new ways. For example,

---

KEY STEP -- RESTATEMENT OF MISSION GOAL.
"What can we add to our chicken that you (or consumers) would pay more for?

Why would consumers want to buy chicken anyway? Why is our chicken different from anyone else's?"

(Ernie) "...because it's fresh."

"What does fresh mean?"

(Sue) "To me, fresh means it's never been frozen. If I were buying fresh chicken, I'd like to know how long the supermarket had the product."

"What could you do to make the consumer aware?"

(Sue) "Maybe a hangtag..."

KEY STEP -- BUILDS ON THE IDEA
"That's interesting, can anyone build on Sue's idea?"

(Ellen) "How about fresh cooked chicken with a lot of seasonings?"

(Bill) "I don't like seasonings..."

(Ellen) "...and no seasonings for Bill."

KEY STEP -- METAPHORS
"Now I'd like you to help me with something different."
Ask any of the brainstormers to choose a word that's on your pad. Than ask each person next to free associate with the previous word. Write all words down.
(Bill) "Fresh..."

(Ellen) "Cooked..."

(Ernie) "Fire..."

(Jeremy) "Ice..."

"Now I want you to close your eyes and force feed any of these words into an image that comes close to the project objective. For instance, how is chicken like fire? What new prepared products can be made with chicken that would be appealing to consumers? What image can you conjure up in your mind -- using any of these words?"

Write down answers.

"Thank you for coming. You've been a great help."

**Figure 2-2.** *(Continued)*

*The problem:* To come up with a new soup that can serve as a base for cooking other meals.

*Restatement:* What kind of foods can be made using a soup base?

*Alternative way of looking at the problem:* Why and what kind of person would use a soup as an ingredient? What occasions would that person use it for?

Instruct the group that no one has any titles in this room and everyone is an equal.

All ideas should be written, by you or an assistant, on the large pad with full pages torn off and taped to the walls to provide your group with further inspiration. Your brainstormers will take the physical act of writing down their ideas as a kind of reward for a job well done. Allow time for respondents to think but not so much that the enthusiasm wanes.

Try to combine ideas whenever possible. A new combination will often create a brand new product. That's the unlikely story of how the circular saw was invented. As she was working on her spinning wheel, a Shaker woman was watching two men ploddingly cut wood with a straight-bladed saw. She realized how much quicker the job would be if saw teeth were cut into the wheel.

Brainstorming is merely formalizing the structure you have at the coffee table or water cooler. During this phase you should be more concerned abut the quantity of ideas rather than the quality. One idea will lead to another until you take it to unimagined places. Premature judgment of ideas is the prime inhibitor. Don't be afraid to go too far out and have your group come up with the wildest ideas imaginable.

At the end of the ideation session you will typically have 50 to 75 seed ideas. Some brainstorming companies suggest you type up the brainstorming charts and circulate them. I heartily recommend against it. I've never seen anything good come out of the practice, and you risk getting a wide array of totally disjointed and off-the-wall ideas into hands of people who have no idea of what you're doing and think it's silly, meaningless, and how come they weren't invited?

The results of a good brainstorm are:

1. All the people at the brainstorming session now have a vested interest in the project so they're on your side.
2. You now have the seeds for developing the new product because you can add what's missing—the human touch.
3. Because now you can evolve or "tweak" the ideas to success.

### What to Eliminate

Now it's time for editing. Many of the concepts will be in the abstract so those can be eliminated. Many will be duplicates. Many will be too far beyond the fringe. The goal will be develop a group of starter concepts that you can expose to consumers.

Don't eliminate ideas for technological reasons (except the obvious ones—like a pill that turns into a full-sized car when you soak it in water). If there's any doubt at all, keep it in. The consumer is going to make the final product decision, and your product idea is going to evolve into something you can make.

*A moneysaving tip:* You don't have to work in a big company or in any company at all to have a brainstorming session. Just your spouse and some friends at an informal gathering over some wine can spur some real excitement. A hint, though—if you use the wine, the excitement and enthusiasm will wear off when the wine does.

### Tips for Better Brainstorming

1. Provide plenty of room and plenty of tape or pushpins to display visual stimuli and ideas.
2. Run the session first thing in the morning, when everyone is bright and chipper. Never do one after lunch.
3. Make sure you set the stage for the meeting beforehand with a written memo outlining objectives.
4. Keep the ideas coming. Keep things moving, but make sure you also allow time to think.
5. Make sure every idea is written down and displayed, no matter how off-the-wall it may seem at the time. You can tame the wilder ideas later.
6. Encourage combining and improving on ideas already given.
7. Don't forget to invite secretaries and mail room personnel. Quite often they have their finger on the pulse of the community that you're too busy to see.
8. Don't bring too much food to an ideation session. It tends to tire people out.
9. If you don't know everyone at the ideation or if everyone is not familiar with each other, name cards can be helpful.

## Summary

1. The idea session is just the first step in developing a new idea. All ideas should be analyzed and acted upon in the hopes of building a strong product opportunity. The goal of an idea session or radical hypothezation is *not to come up with a winning idea but a seed on which to build a winning idea.*
2. All successful new-product ideas must be able to be described in a sentence or less. Consumers don't have any more time than that.
3. Applied creativity can be sparked in three simple words:

   Immerse
   Forget
   Stimulate

4. It is necessary to explore all polarities of the new-product spectrum to implement a thorough and effective ideation program. It's easier to edit out an unworkable idea than to generate a brand new one.
5. Don't outsmart yourself and eliminate ideas too soon.

## Questions, Answers, and Additional Insights

*But I already have the new product idea. Why do I need to brainstorm?*
To verify your idea and to make it even better. Like the dog following its tail, the human mind is constantly chasing after itself, following the same circular reasoning processes. Brainstorming provides additional material for you to evaluate. In effect, you'll be developing new stimuli and new alternatives to react to, allowing you to improve your judgment because you will be considering more things. There's no shortage of people who will tell you that your idea is the best. Avoid them at all costs. Self-delusion is incredibly expensive. But there's also no shortage of people who will tell you that your idea is the worst. Avoid them at all costs also, for nothing is more expensive to the soul than discouragement. The best way is to get a collection of ideas on the table so better judgments can be made.

*I don't consider myself a creative person, just a business person. What makes a creative person?*
The creative and rational functions are more related than most of us believe. The schism develops when people try to separate the two ar-

bitrarily. Time after time I have sat across from marketing managers or even (gulp!) lawyers or accountants who tell me that they aren't creative and then they proceed to peal off one idea after another. Many people don't like to admit being creative. Creativity is showmanship of the mind. It's where we get to put our thoughts on stage the same way a singer or ballplayer does. Many people are afraid to bare their creative impulses. When you don't get the needed applause, you stop performing. A major company did a controlled study on the differences between people who were considered creative and those who were not. The major difference was that creative people were not afraid to fail. Those people didn't censor their minds.

*How can I get my people to be responsive?*
New-product ideas can and should come from everyone and everywhere. Just create an atmosphere in which every idea will be taken seriously and considered at some point in the idea search. Conduct informal brain-picking sessions at the coffee machine and with anyone who expresses the slightest interest.

*Should the idea or the product come first?*
It can work either way. If your product is "off-the-shelf," then the mission is to explore for viability and possible improvements. Brainstorming sessions should entail new positioning, marketing strategies, and distribution routes. If you're looking for the new-product opportunities, then you should start from scratch and hypothesize consumer wants and desires first.

# 3
# The Art of Positioning Your New Product

*Chapter preview:*

- ***How to find a consumer need and make sure your product fulfills it***
- ***The 5 Ws and the H to new-product success***
- ***Performance cues—proving to your customer that your product works***
- ***Why selling to everyone ultimately leads to failure***
- ***Why one-sentence solutions work better than a laundry list of claims***
- ***How to find the most receptive market for your product, and vice versa***

Successful new product development is about need fulfillment and wish fulfillment (not yours, the consumer's) and a receptive audience—the target market. Like the product, the positioning should be constantly monitored, constantly evolved. Chapters 3 and 4 will help you take the guesswork out of product positioning and focus on what and who is really important—the ultimate user, or consumer.

"Wait a second," you're probably saying, "why are we talking about positioning when we don't even have a product yet?"

Why wait? Your winning positioning is the consumer hook that will make your target consumer seek out your product above all others, so why wait until the product is built to recognize your opportunities or mistakes? Doesn't it make sense to construct your product around a winning positioning and to make it an integral part of your product? Trout and Ries, in a classic positioning book, call positioning the "battle for your mind." But it's more than just an advertising slogan on a media shingle. Much more.

Today's products are thrust into an intensely competitive "sell or die" marketing environment. We don't usually have the luxury of tinkering once the product is on the shelf. Packaging, formulations, and advertising are just too expensive. We have to make sure we have the right product for the right audience. We have to target everything perfectly—before we hit the marketplace.

A benefit is only perceived as useful when the consumer recognizes that a need exists. When you offer benefits to someone who does not even realize he or she has a concern, the benefit will be ignored. Product features don't create an interest. The benefits to the consumer are what matters and drives the product.

Positioning is all the news about how your product relates to the consumer in one brief sentence. It's the single-minded selling proposition that makes your product stand out in a consumer's life. Contrary to most traditional thought (and since most new products fail, traditional thought is apparently wrong) the positioning of the potential product benefits should be determined at the earliest stages of the new-product development process, because it should determine all aspects of your product.

Positioning is *not* an add-on, to be relegated to the vicissitudes and whims of an advertising agency who, more often than not, is looking for a rationalization for an ad campaign. Despite what your advertising agency might say, when it talks about new products and positioning, it is usually just guessing.

Remember working on the school newspaper, when you were taught the 5 *W*s and the *H*? How brevity, conciseness, and intensity of the lead were the key?

If you never had journalism, the 5 *W*s and the *H* were not a rock group or even the defensive alignment of the Washington Redskins but a one-sentence solution to getting to the hearts and minds of the reader.

For new-product developers, they are:

*W*ho is the product for?

*W*hat will the product do for the consumer?

*W*hy would the consumer want it?

*W*hen should that person use it?

*W*here should the product be used? Where would it be found (in what store, where in the store)?

*H*ow does it work? Most importantly, how will it affect the purchaser's life?

(See Fig. 3-1.)

## More Is Less—Really!

As mentioned in the last chapter, if you can't sell the product in a single sentence, you really don't have a product, no matter how excited R&D gets. Whenever you take longer than that, you actually dilute the message. Having five mediocre product benefits is not nearly as effective as having one strong one. An all-purpose cooking sauce, no matter how

Who is the product for? ______________________

______________________________________________

What will it do for the consumer? ______________

______________________________________________

Why would the consumer want it? Or use it? ______

______________________________________________

When is the product to be used? ________________

______________________________________________

Where should it be used? ______________________

______________________________________________

How is it going to affect the consumer's life...for the better? ______________________________________

______________________________________________

**Figure 3-1.** The 5 *W*s and the *H* of product positioning. How does your product measure up?

good it tastes, is not nearly as powerful a seller as a spaghetti sauce. Do you go to the store looking for an all-purpose sauce or one that makes baked ziti taste good?

The 5 *W*s and the *H* are the keys to a winning new-product positioning. They function as the heart of your new-product strategy and provide an ongoing checklist to make sure your new product is focused throughout the process.

My favorite positioning story involves a two-line ad I created for the secretary of a client. Her husband was trying to sell his Jeep that had a snow plow attachment. He had run numerous ads in the auto and truck sections of various newspapers talking about the virtues of the vehicle—low mileage, new tires, great engine—typical car stuff. No response.

We ran the following ad in the Business Opportunity section of the local Pennysaver: "Start your own snow removal business—Late model jeep with plow. Excellent money making potential." The Jeep sold the first day. The power of positioning.

### Slice of Life

I was part of the team that made First Brand's Glad Lock Bags a major part of the U.S. scene. Actually it was an innovative positioning, rather than the product itself, that made it a major success. First Brands (then Union Carbide) had developed a new zipper-top bag to challenge Dow's Ziplock bags. The concept of the bag was simple. One side of the closure was yellow. One side was blue. When you closed the seal, it became green—we're talking basic third-grade color-wheel logic here.

R&D was delighted with the concept, but consumers were underwhelmed. When it was shown to housewives—the key target market—the product was positioned as the bag that was so easy to close, "you'll get it right every time." Housewives were unanimous in considering the product silly, gimmicky, and of meaningless significance. But as they shook their heads no, consumers kept playing with the bag.

R&D and the sponsoring marketing managers were crushed. But since response was so strong, although negative, we knew we were on to something.

We made a minor positioning change to "The bag that is so simple, even husbands and kids get it right every time." It struck an immediate chord with women. "Yeah, my husband's a slob and my kids never wrap up things correctly." The change allowed the consumer to rationalize the expense and gimmickry of the color change features.

Until we presented the positioning and the problem it solved, most consumers weren't even aware that they had the problem! The positioning solved a need that consumers didn't even know they had!

The positioning change made marketing history and took First Brands —the company that spun off of Union Carbide's Consumer Marketing Division—out of massive debt.

In the United States, fortunately, most of our physical needs are met—air, food, water. The complexities of human nature, illogical human behavior, and the desire to be dazzled are why consumers are eager to try and embrace a new product when it fulfills a perceived human need.

## A Successful Product Should Sell Itself Four Times

Any good new product should sell itself four times in order to obtain and keep the consumer's loyalty:

1. *On the shelf or in the store.* The product should beckon the consumer past all the products surrounding it, acting like a beacon on the shelf.

2. *At the checkout.* The product must continue to attract the consumer at this final "decision point" and avoid the consumer's "cut list."
3. *In use.* The product should perform in such a way that reinforces the positioning.
4. *After use.* Like a great entertainer, the product should leave the consumer wanting more!

*Perception is what the consumer believes (or wants to believe) about your product. Consumer perception is the reality, even if it's mistaken.*

Let's look at today's computer software, for example. In ancient times, before Columbus discovered America, people would type letters and reports on their trusty IBM Selectrics or even on (dread) manual typewriters. (Let's face it. Before somebody demonstrated the usefulness of the typewriter, and created that need, people were very happy with a quill pen.) Then, along came two Californians who said, a day or so after getting clobbered by one too many surfboards, "Let's invent the home computer." The personal computer eventually begat word processing software.

So that's how Wordstar word processing software got started—the most complicated piece of "help" ever invented by humans to, essentially, aid someone in putting down 26 letters in recognizable patterns.

Eventually, software evolved and became more "user friendly." (That's software talk for not having to press down 16 keys to get a capital G.) The people who ran software companies learned what features people really needed to be useful for their everyday writing. The software manufacturers became more selective in what they put into their software and removed some of the more esoteric and little used functions.

Naturally, the stripped-down versions didn't sell very well. People continue to buy the most feature-packed software, even if they can't figure out how to use it. Software consumers want to feel they could write the great American novel, even though no writer I know who actually writes for a living wants all the features, because they tend to get in the way.

Japanese automakers were baffled when their U.S. subsidiaries requested that they install compact disk players in their luxury cars. The manufacturers argued that road noise and interior noise would drown out the high and low end notes that CDs delivered so faithfully. The subsidiaries argued, successfully, that the CD would appeal to the U.S. buyer who wanted the best and that the CD would reinforce the quality perception of the vehicles. It would be a contributing factor in closing the deal. They were right. It didn't make one bit of difference that the performance potential of the CD would be unfulfilled. The fact that the car had a CD at all added to the gestalt of the luxury car experience. It allowed the buyer to brag, either verbally or silently, "Look what I got." Can auto microwaves be far behind?

## How Should Positioning Be Manifested?

Positioning can be about something as basic and simple as coloring and flavoring your product and delivering performance cues. Positioning products for different market segments gives you a dearth of product opportunities. Camera manufacturers have learned to differentiate their products in a number of ways—for instance, making the basic camera in bright hues and fun colors targeting snapshooters who want simplicity in taking pictures of friends and family. But the manufacturers also make cameras with buttons, lights, and supergizmos for the photographers who *think* they're more sophisticated.

Remember George Eastman, way back in Chapter 1? One of the first Kodak cameras he sold back in the 1900s came fully loaded with film. "Press the button, we do the rest" was the slogan. The user had to send the camera back to the lab with the film to be developed.

The hottest camera today? The Kodak disposable, positioned for a fast, on-the-go lifestyle. You have to send the camera back to the lab, with the film, to be developed. Same song. Different words.

How important is positioning? Several years ago, a professional photographer took the identical pictures under the same lighting conditions and circumstances with every major brand of 35 millimeter camera. The photos were identical. Yet people still swear that the Nikon performs better, because it's the camera for "professionals."

Swatch watches turned the watch market upside down, and the formerly declining Swiss watch industry right-side-up with its line of inexpensive, colorful sport watches. They were simply—sorry Timex, you missed the boat—fun. Swatch found its market and built its product around it. Believe it or not, the original Swatch watches are now considered "classics" and command super-high prices from collectors.

### Priorities, Priorities, Priorities

Too often, even the most experienced marketers get caught up with who they are and what they can make rather than with what the consumer will buy from them. Atari created a beautifully engineered computer about the same time IBM introduced its PC. The Atari never took off. Computer aficionados still equated Atari with Space Invaders and arcade-type games—a reputation the company has never been able to shake. Commodore computers, at one time, virtually owned the U.S. home computer business. They slid past everyone with their low-priced Commodore 64 (I had five of them). They lost their edge when they tried to expand their U.S. business market. They never developed bragging rights like IBM and Apple and it hurt them. Would you like to be the one to tell your boss you've ordered Commodores and Ataris for the office, rather than IBM? Researching the product and positioning for their products in the beginning stages of their programs would have saved these companies vast sums of developmental costs and allowed them to focus on making much-needed corrections.

Positioning opportunities are constantly changing and evolving due to new events and the constant fluctuations of the consumer mindset. When I started writing this chapter, cholesterol was the "Killer Nightmare from Food Hell." This morning I heard that cholesterol wasn't too bad, but watch those fats. And just last week I heard that drinking moderately was good for me.

### The Positioning Continuum

Recently, while interviewing a teenage girl, I asked her what car she would buy if money were no object. She told me a Dodge Stealth, an upscale sports car. Probing her further, she said that if she had the money, she would really buy a Chevrolet Beretta, a somewhat lower-priced sports car. I asked why, and she said that the Stealth was too good and that she was afraid of getting it dirty and scratched.

When I asked her if that was the real reason, she said, "not really." She said that the Stealth was almost too good for her. She didn't have an ego problem, but her friends would think she was uppity and conceited. It would look like she was trying to show off. She might even be too self-conscious to drive it into the high school parking lot.

We—all consumers, in fact—are guided by our limitations as well as our aspirations. Many of these limitations are internally imposed. For instance, if we secretly think the car is too good for us, we may rationalize it by telling people we're afraid of dents, whereas in reality the car tweaks our self-image a bit too much. Perhaps we're afraid of our wives' reactions to our splurge. Our peers' reaction to our spending misjudgment is also a major factor. Or if the car was less than we really wanted, we may make an unrelated excuse that's nonthreatening to our ego—the small car made it unsafe for my family, etc.

These fall into a positioning continuum (Fig. 3-2) which defines the positioning limits of your product. Here's an example of developing a

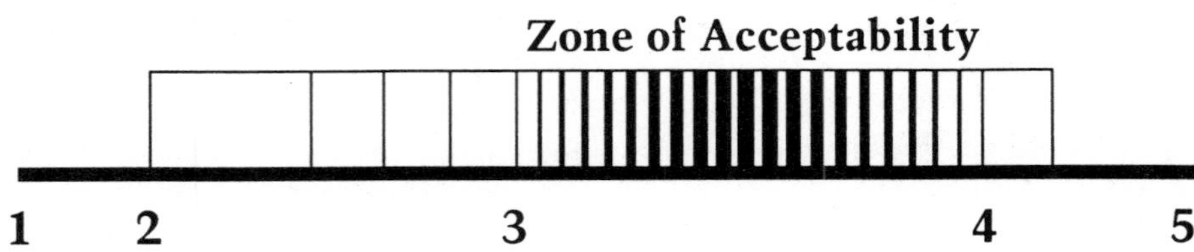


**Figure 3-2.** The positioning continuum defines the positioning range of your product. The greatest competition tends to cluster in the center. 1 = too downscale—outside perceived personal/financial limits; 2 = barely acceptable (often price-intensive); 3 = acceptable; 4 = truly desired; 5 = too upscale—outside perceived personal/financial limits.

product based on the positioning continuum: A marketer of alcoholic beverages showed me a bottle of 20-year-old scotch in a beautiful decanter marketed at $200 a bottle. "How many bottles of this do you expect to sell?" I asked.

"None," he said.

"But why...."

"When scotch drinkers see the $200 bottle which is totally beyond their reach, they'll switch to the $30 bottle made by the same company, and suddenly that becomes affordable, if not a downright bargain. You see, it's got the same gold motif, the same decanter shape." Borrowing or transferring interest is an excellent way of positioning your product.

A good new-product positioning achieves the fine balance between the emotional and physical and shouts it from the shelf.

## Positioning by End Use

In the over-the-counter drug business, unique single-minded, one-sentence positionings have been panaceas for drug regulations. Nyquil is an excellent example of positional marketing. The Richardson-Vicks people have actually taken a side-effect of most cold preparations—getting drowsy—and made a benefit of it by saying it helps you ignore the cold symptoms and get to sleep. After over a decade the product is still going strong. Now it comes in kid's strengths and flavors. It even comes in a capsule without alcohol, even though alcohol was another key ingredient in Nyquil that helped you get to sleep.

Diphenhydramine—an antihistamine for colds and allergies—is also being hawked as a sleeping aid in Sominex and other over-the-counter sleeping preparations. And yes, it's an ingredient in Nyquil Liquicaps. Will the cleverness never cease?

### Positioning by Taking Advantage of Your Limitations

At one time, Cornish hens were a little-sought gourmet item. They were too expensive or a bit too luxurious to make the weekly dinner plate. It was outside the consumer's personal zone of acceptance. Producers then repositioned the birds as a midweek, convenient, affordable luxury. The producers successfully moved it into the consumer's zone of acceptability.

Plain old aspirin has been positioned in hundreds of different ways. Seltzered, flaked, as a liquid, as a gum, the aspirin is the same in every one of them.

Packaging can also serve as a mnemonic device for the written statement—a headline without words. Contadina has introduced a line of fresh food wrapped in good old clear plastic wrap. With other companies jumping on the Saran Wrap-like bandwagon, Saran Wrap is becoming the instant way to position your product as fresh.

### Positioning According to the Competition

A quick study at the supermarket or the department store can help you find a preemptive market niche. Exploring the positioning range of simple products like wine or candy can help you come up with a wide variety of physical, emotional, or pricing attributes.

Coor's Brewing Company has introduced Keystone Beer—"bottled beer taste that comes in a can," whatever that means. And Miller Beer has recycled that bromide positioning—"draft beer taste, now in a can," whatever that means.

#### Slice of Life

Planters Life Savers wanted to open up a new product area for its mixed nuts. It explored the competition and the shelves and came up with a selection of nuts, called Good Measure, positioned strictly for baking. Planters packaged them in resealable canisters instead of cellophane bags, which was the traditional way cooking nuts were packaged. Planters emphasized to bakers and aisle browsers that the portions were premeasured. In keeping with the positioning, Planters used a measuring cup design on the package. It chalked up a 45 percent increase in baking segment sales, strictly due to this unique repositioning. Simple. Obvious. Smart.

### Niche and Segmentation Opportunities

I don't think that I'm out of line suggesting most of us don't have the resources and money of a Lever Brothers or a Kellogg's. So we can't market like them. It's often essential to go after niches or market segments that are being ignored by the giants. Each marketing segment is an individual opportunity with its own unique needs that you can fulfill. These can be identified by demographics, economics, geographical boundaries, and lifestyles. While beverage makers around the country were taking caffeine out of coffee and cola, Jolt cola and Buzz coffee were developed with twice the normal caffeine.

A strong positioning seeks out its own customer. A major problem that marketers (especially novice marketers) face is trying to sell to everyone. Everyone doesn't want anything. Trying to pick off a concentrated consumer segment is more efficient than going after everyone.

## Positioning as a Way to Add Value in the Consumer's Mind

Positioning opportunities are more than the sum of the ingredients in a product. They're new businesses, provided they're marketed that way. In order to position and segment the market, think of positioning not as narrowing down your potential market or audience but as a *value-added proposition,* reaching for a new user who is reaching for a new product.

Miller Lite was the first "light" beer to show real athletes—people whom beer drinkers could identify with in real life settings—drinking a light beer. It defined the consumer's perception of what a light beer—and what a light beer drinker—should be. You could be macho and still drink light.

Miller, with a macho light beer claim, changed the rules of the game, and light beer soon dominated the business. Even beers that were already *seen* as light, particularly by their manufacturers, such as Coors of Colorado, had to reformulate to be *called* Light.

Because of the two-paycheck family and the acceptance of the prepared dinner, the individuals in the family unit are getting choices. Mom and Dad can get fat-free entrees and the kids can pig out on frozen lasagna. These are strong potential positioning opportunities.

A strong positioning can even drive consumers into a category. Figure 3-3 illustrates how an inexpensive item that some formerly called junk food changes in appeal when we attach a fat-free label on it. Now, it's not just for kids but for baby boomers grabbing a quick bite. It's essentially a new product for a new audience. Surprisingly, the new audience is the baby boomer who can get a quick, guilt-free junk food fix.

At a recent trade show, there were some very interesting products. One entrepreneur had created a line of liquid spices. The packaging was interesting, and the flavors proved excellent. There was one problem. When asked what the positioning of the product was, she had no clue.

**Figure 3-3.** This "light" positioning drove new, older consumers back into the snack food category.

She had no idea why a consumer should purchase it and even less reasons for a retailer to stock it. She came up with five intellectual reasons to buy, but not one was strong enough to put on a label or capture the attention of someone wandering through a store.

At the same trade show, two entrepreneurs had similar pasta snack products. I asked what the difference was. Each independently launched into tech-talk about mouth feel and textures and how difficult the products were to manufacture. Yet, neither could differentiate one product from the other on the shelf, in the store, or in any way at all.

At the same show there were a number of ready-made iced cappucinos, so many to sample that I was almost in a caffeine frenzy. Then I stopped at the only one that was in a milk-type container instead of a metal can. "What's the difference?" I asked, somewhat intrigued.

"It's made fresh, from fresh milk, so it tastes natural." The package said, somewhat ingenuously, "shake and froth." What positioning could be more succinct and ignite a cappucino drinker's taste buds? No song and dance about how they did it, but this one-sentence positioning separated it from every other product at the show.

There are over ten thousand products in the average store, and the consumer has to make a snap decision about every one of them. Consumers are constantly changing their frames of reference and their zones of acceptability as the market and the media cause them to alter their opinions and judgments:

- A convenience food now is an instant food, requiring 10 minutes or less in a microwave.
- A frozen dinner that you have to oven cook now has some of the old-fashioned cachet of food your grandmother used to make.

- The standard identity of a milk shake is not the kind that came out of fountains but the ersatz glop you get at McDonalds or Burger King.

- $1.50 is now acceptable to pay for a chocolate cookie, but $2.00 is too high. People will pay $1.99 for a tube of toothpaste but not $2.09. That's why, despite the efforts of *Consumer Reports,* the $0.95 and $0.99 price point will never go away.

### Positioning Helps the Trade Too

Retailers also want to take advantage of the path of least resistance. They won't spend time trying to figure out your marketing strategy for you. They will put your product next to similar products in the store. That's why a strong positioning creates a geographic niche in the store.

### What Positioning Won't Do

Although proper positioning is vital to a successful new product, all the positioning in the world won't save a poor product or a product that doesn't deliver. Indeed, it will make the product fail faster when people rush to buy your product and it doesn't perform as advertised. Consumers will usually give your new product one audition. If it doesn't solve their needs, they're quick to cross you off their shopping list.

One major company has been attempting to reposition an ultrafamous brand name cleaning product. The advertising promoted strong trial. Then consumers who bought the product experienced a major disappointment. The product didn't work as well as it used to. Consumers tried the product and found there was nothing behind the famous brand name anymore. It turns out, in order to keep the balance sheets looking good, the manufacturer had been removing the active ingredients. And these are the same manufacturers who complain about lack of brand loyalty.

Positioning won't sell a product if it doesn't fulfill someone's perceived needs or when it creates problems that didn't exist before. An example was Kimberly Clark's bathroom wipes. These were premoistened wipes that were impregnated with disinfectant cleaner for the bathroom. Here are some of the problems the product created:

- The trade didn't know where to stock it. Should it be placed near the cleaners or the paper towels?
- Consumers didn't know how to use it, where to place it in the bathroom, or where to find it in the store. And suppose the bathroom had a wet stain? Did the consumer use a dry paper towel, a damp sponge,

or the bathroom wipes? In a typically cramped bathroom, where would the consumer find room to store the product?

### How Do You Find the Product to Fulfill a Positioning Opportunity?

Work on the positioning of your product from the very beginning. Chapter 5 goes through the various research steps in detail, but briefly, here is how to make sure your positioning is on target in the zone of acceptability before you make your costly materials investment. Taking a little extra time now to make sure your positioning is on the mark can make all the difference in your final bottom line. Experiment on paper before you spend on materials. Paper is cheaper than molds.

1. Based on the ideas developed from your ideation sessions, make a starter list of possible product superiority objectives (positionings) by guessing at hypothetical consumer problems you can solve. If your product already exists, make the list of benefits and possible adaptations (never show a feature without the putative consumer benefit) pertinent to your product.
2. Place these on realistic examples of ads (concepts) that graphically cover the positionings. (See Fig. 3-4.) Try to include pricing.
3. Now show these ads to consumers. Keep revising and changing your positionings (as you revise your product) and show them to consumers over and over again, until you strike a consumer nerve—until you come up with the one sentence positioning that consumers get truly excited about. Consumers must get excited and understand all the key elements of your product just by looking at the ad.

Your winning positioning strategy is now a road map that will guide R&D, packaging, engineering, and other divisions. And it will probably impress the heck out of your company president, or boss.

Once you establish the positioning and criteria for your product, you can create the product. If you have a product, you can establish the criteria for your positioning, packaging, and communications.

## Summary

1. Remember the basic goal of your positioning is to make consumers feel a little better about themselves for buying and using your product. It's a vital link between your product and the consumer.

*(Text continues on page 69.)*

**Figure 3-4.** The same product, but many different ways of looking at it (pages 60 to 68). Notice that the packaging and product name are considered a key part of the concept.

**Figure 3-4.** (*Continued*)

**Figure 3-4.** (*Continued*)

**Figure 3-4.** *(Continued)*

**Figure 3-4.** (*Continued*) (Notice the illustrations and expanded usage claims!)

**Figure 3-4.** *(Continued)*

**Figure 3-4.** (*Continued*)

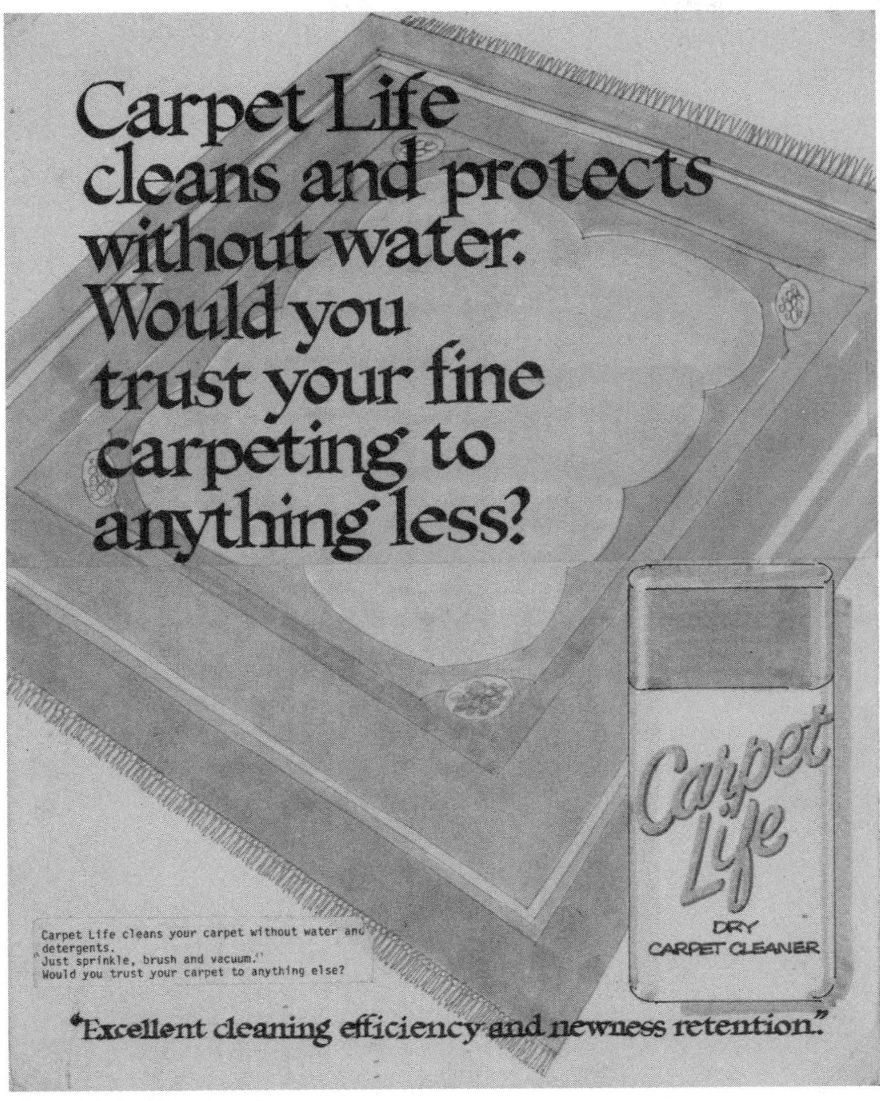


**Figure 3-4.** (*Continued*)

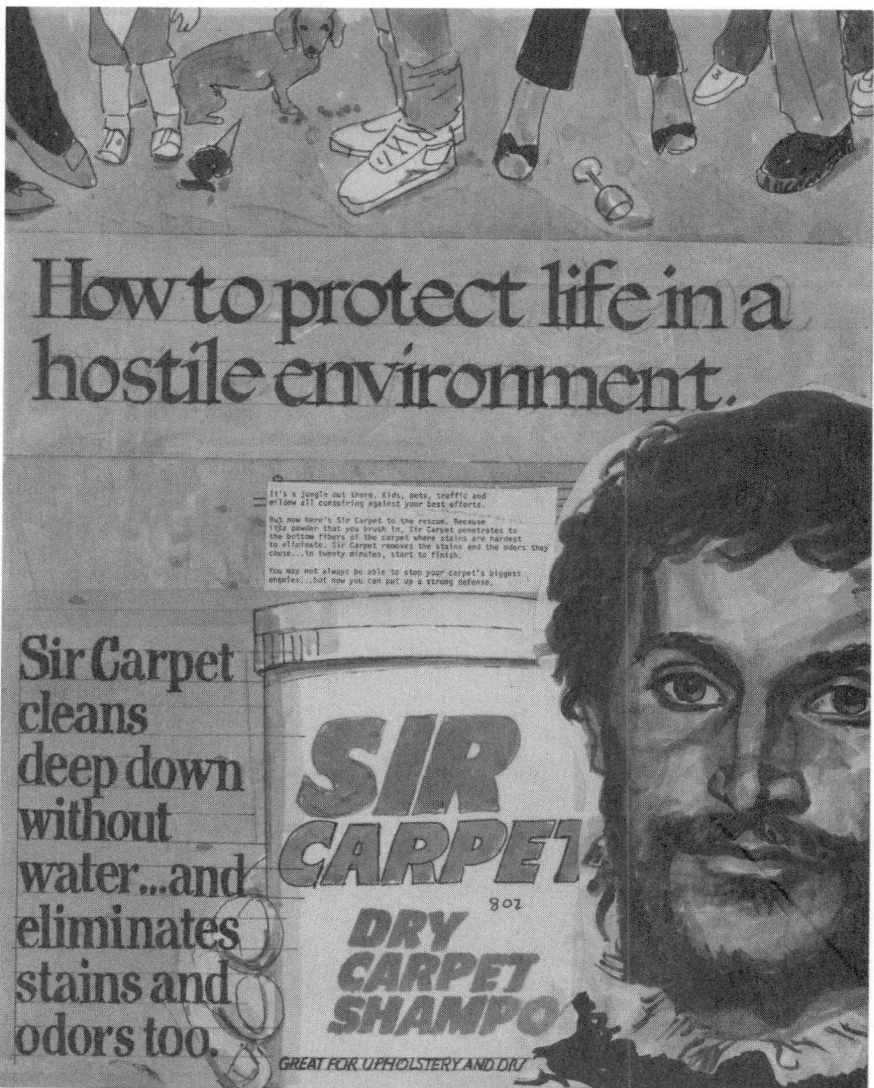


**Figure 3-4.** (*Continued*)

2. The 5 *W*s and the *H* are the keys to winning new product strategy.
3. A new positioning for an older product can be more effective in terms of sales than an exciting, breakthrough-type product with no clear-cut positioning.
4. The positioning of your product should be fully thought through at the beginning of the new product process (even in the initial ideation) rather than added as an afterthought.

## Questions, Answers, and Additional Insights

*Why is positioning so important?*
Positioning is important because it targets new users for your product while it satisfies existing users. In many product categories a phenomenon called the Pareto principle exists (named after the heretofore obscure nineteenth-century economist Vilfredo Pareto). This principle states that just 20 percent of your customers will account for 80 percent of your sales. Razor-sharp positionings make sure you hone in and satisfy these markets.

*How does positioning work in a business-to-business situation?*
In business-to-business marketing, positioning is even more important because there are more variables due to all the layers of management one has to sell through. Each management layer acts as a filtering device preventing you from contacting your key targets. Your prospect's personnel, from secretaries to the president, immediately want to know how you fit in their total picture. By positioning yourself, your company, and your product to fit their needs you can get through a great deal of the negativity and skepticism and separate yourself from the competition. Surprisingly, the same influences go into a buyer buying a computer as a consumer buying a toothbrush. Rarely is it just the power of your unit or prices—the decision to buy often rests on a hot button or a gut feeling.

*What if the physical components of the product or the technology have not caught up with the positioning?*
This is a particularly sticky question and causes numerous disputes between marketing and R&D. Yet it shouldn't be a problem. The positioning and the physical aspects of the products are complementary but separate (although to the consumer they are one and the same). If

you can't change the product, then change the positioning. For instance, at this moment, many companies are trying to develop fat- and cholesterol-reduced food substitutes. None of these has been able to mimic the exact mouth feel of fats and oils. The problem companies are having is attempting to position these fat- and cholesterol-reduced products, in the consumer's mind, as an equivalent to the real thing. The product's don't, and can't, measure up. The companies should be developing new positionings and expectations in the consumers' minds by having the fat-free products stand on their own. With new positionings, these new tastes and textures may be quite acceptable. Constant experimentation with new positionings, as well as new product executions is vital from the very beginning of the project. That's why we recommend that all departments work together from the outset and why we think the common practice of putting R&D and marketing in separate buildings is ludicrous.

*So how do you separate the product from the positioning?*
Without a doubt, that's the question I get asked the most. You don't. The key to developing a successful new product is to exploit a niche, a feeling, a need, a product benefit. Consumers don't separate the product from the benefit. Why should you?

*How do I become a positioning whiz?*
Keep your mind and your eyes open. Positioning opportunities are virtually limitless. Here are some starting points: You can position on physical product characteristics, demographics, user characteristics, product usage, standards of evaluation, benefits, pricing, image (although this is directly related to "share of heart"), physical needs, lifestyles, and heritage.

*Are there any shortcuts to developing a positioning strategy?*
You can quickly define your positioning with licensed characters, downsizing your product, upsizing it, making it more portable, using pricing, etc. In all these cases, the product form will dictate visually how it will be used.

# 4

# You Gotta Have Share of Heart

***Chapter preview:***

- ***"Share of heart" explained and defined***
- ***Why it can make or break your product***
- ***How it totally defies logic and why bottled water is so damned expensive***
- ***Why share of heart should be determined in the developmental product stages, not after***
- ***Why an intangible called imagery is so important***
- ***Tested, proven ways to get consumers emotionally involved in your product***

If positioning is the heart of new-product development success, then "share of heart" is the soul of your new-product venture. Here's where the magic enters. Here's where you tell the consumer there's something very special about your product. Here's where you put all the elements of your product together and make it something of great personal value.

Choose one of two scenarios:

1. Your hot new product idea is in the works, and you lie awake at 4:00 a.m. waiting for the prototype to arrive. You've even picked out your his-and-hers Porsches with the slideaway roofs and built in VCRs. Of course, you've done all your homework and think, "If just one in one hundred people buy my product, I'll be a zillionaire." To you it only makes sense; how can anyone *not* want this product?
2. It's still 4:00 a.m., and you stare at the smudge on your ceiling. Earlier, you passed a display in a store that has a product that looks just like yours. Ultimate despair. It's only logical, you think. If someone beat me to the marketplace, then what's the use of launching my product? You hastily update your résumé.

In both cases, close your eyes and remember: Consumers are neither rational nor consistent in their purchase behavior. If they were, we'd all be rich.

## Why Do People Buy One Product over Another?

*The logical reason:* The product provides better features or benefits than another. It fulfills perceived *physical* needs at a price the consumer is willing to pay. *The real reason:* The personality and image of the product meet human needs with *emotionally* satisfying benefits, even though the product itself may seem to betray common sense. It's called "share of heart." *Share of heart* is the emotional link your product shares with a prospective consumer. Share of heart is the single most important aspect of creative marketing—as important as the big Idea.

As proof of this, look at the U.S. fascination with spectator sports. It defies reason. We don't root for a player, although the player may have transient relevance, as much as we root for a logo—a brand name. The players, making three million dollars a year or more and having no identification with their fans, may change from one year to the next. They can be traded, dropped from the team, or play for another team, yet we continue to root for the team.

Share of heart answers the two key questions that are a part of almost any purchase. How is the product going to reach out and touch this person? How is your product going to improve the consumer's life? Share of heart is also about adding a touch of salesmanship and personality to your product through subtle cues.

Suppose you had a beverage that consumers could get virtually free or buy for a few cents. Now, suppose that consumers were told they would have the opportunity to purchase the product elsewhere for $3.50—or more than three hundred times your price—and consumers purchased the product in droves. You'd laugh. You'd probably be somewhat peeved, too. Especially if the product was something as basic as water. But that's exactly what is being done with bottled water. It's a $2 billion industry built on nothing but water and pure unadulterated emotion.

Share of heart, like positioning, is how consumers perceive that your product enhances their lifestyle and self-image, how the product bonds with the consumer. You've been hearing the words *perceives* and *perception* a lot in this book. In marketing, perception is the reality. For instance, even though experts find that the best of the bottled waters offers no real improvement in taste, substance, or healthiness over many metro tap waters, consumers continue to imbibe at champagne prices. They attach almost mythical properties to their favorites. To stretch credibility even further, restaurants are pouring it over ice cubes made with—guess what?—tap water.

Sellers of bottled water know they're selling more than something as basic as $H_2O$. They're selling an image. For a relatively small amount of money, the users feel they're doing something for themselves—perhaps adding a little safe celebration to life, or perhaps treating themselves to a little luxury, or even a little social one-upsmanship. Let's face it. It looks good and chic to be seen carrying the unique Evian bottle. By treating water as a fashionable "accessory" rather than a basic commodity, Evian's marketers have bonded it to a well-defined segment of consumers and are challenging Perrier (who, with its little green bottle, virtually created the business) for leadership. [A side point: "Evian" spelled backward is "naive" (just thought you'd like to know).]

One of the reasons much new-product work goes awry is that marketers try to separate the perception from the product features, particularly in the testing stages. To consumers, perception of features is key.

A famous textile cooperative, for instance, actually separated its product into 89 different tangible physical characteristics and tested each of them separately—flexibility, ability to retain water, and on and on. It never quite understood that consumers wanted the product because they perceived it as natural, luxurious, and upscale. To consumers it was more expensive and well worth it. Based on its research, the cooperative's advertising is now essentially a hodgepodge of nondescript product benefits and a total waste of money.

The real skirmish is over the consumers's heart rather than head. Touch the heart and the head will follow. That's the reason professional wrestling works as well as it does. Professional wrestling measures its appeal in cheers and boos. Logic really doesn't enter into it, and the promoters don't allow it to. Customers willingly suspend belief to be entertained.

Want more proof? It seems like everybody's on some kind of diet or "sweatin' to the oldies" at his or her health club. But Haagen Daz, Ben and Jerry's, and the other superrich, super-butterfat, cardiac-blocking ice creams are selling well. The ability of humans to rationalize their pleasures is endless when we help them create the excuse.

## Quality and Perception of Quality Are Not the Same

There's a delicate balance between the physical and the emotional. Having a product that works better or does a new consumer trick is not enough anymore. You've got to feed the ego. Consumers need to feel good about themselves to fulfill their own self-images. It's a basic, human emotional need. You are what you buy.

Like positioning, share of heart should be determined while the product is in the developmental stages, not after. It encompasses more than just advertising because long after the budget is exhausted and the coupons run out, your product is going to have to continue to sell itself.

Of course, physical needs must be met if you're going to have a long-term winner—maybe. But, as we've seen, if emotional benefits and physical benefits are pretty much tied, then the product with emotional benefits wins. Ah, the frustrations of the marketer who has a winner in the lab and in the taste tests but is losing big on the shelves.

Admittedly, it can be hard to go against the existing mindset. Especially when your sales force—or worse, you—thinks it knows more about what consumers want than the consumers themselves. Share of heart should be a part of every aspect of your product from its appearance, how it works, performance cues, packaging, even aromas and portion sizes.

Share of heart is made, not born. It's where you snatch the ultimate victory from the jaws of defeat. It's where you prove to all the harbingers of disaster (such as the reluctant banker) that they were wrong.

### Slice of Life

Let's see why the president of Smartfood broke all the rules in the snack food market and came up with the country's top-selling snack food after starting out trying to market a new kind of reclosable bag. We'll see why, instead of spending their money on advertising, the three original entrepreneurial partners hired people to prance up and down New England ski slopes dressed as giant popcorn bags.

First, an overview of the situation: Three good friends developed a new kind of resealable bag which they were going to market. Logically, they thought, it would be easier to demonstrate the bag if they filled it with something. So, after much back-and-forthing among the partners, they decided—no one is quite sure why—to put popcorn in the bag.

They wanted their popcorn to be different from anyone else's, so they cooked up some cheddar-cheese-flavored popcorn and concocted a story that said it was from an old family recipe. This didn't work too well. There were a lot of cheese-flavored popcorns and no shortage of hackneyed family recipe stories either.

But the Smartfood people came up with an unusual twist. Instead of the usual ersatz popcorn colors that dominated the market, Smartfood kept their popcorn pristinely white. It now had a unique point of difference—a share of heart that separated it from the competitors.

After deciding to do away with the reclosable bag (talk about staying flexible) they rebelled against typical industry packaging colors. They packaged their product in black and yellow so that it stood out from all the other snacks. The whole thing looked very hip. It was a difference they could readily exploit.

But they were almost out of money by this time, so they proceeded to do counterculture marketing. Instead of calling on distributors and wholesalers and spending big money on an advertising blitz, they hired people dressed as giant popcorn bags to give out samples on ski slopes and beaches. They rented an airplane trailing three large bedsheets sewn together with the Smartfood logo. They created a demand that forced retailers to stock their product.

In short, by doing everything the opposite of their mass market competitors, they created a unique, hip, share of heart and became the MTV of snack foods. As an epilogue, they recently sold out to Frito-Lay, the most traditional of snack food marketers.

Every major marketer has products in their archives—good, well-performing products—that failed in the marketplace because they didn't achieve share of heart. The emotional connection or bond to consumers was never made. Atari and Commodore's business computers and 7-Up Gold were all marketing mistakes (well-financed marketing mistakes). They went for physical benefits rather than emotional cues.

And every major marketer was also envious at the success of the three women who marketed the incredibly successful Epilady hair remover—the product that logic could not kill. How far will a consumer go when you strike an emotional chord? How can an appliance that yanks hair out, strand by strand, from women's legs succeed? The Epilady did this, on purpose no less, and women stormed the stores to buy it.

### Slice of Life

Let me backtrack. The Epilady was invented by two Israeli engineers in 1985 and marketed in Europe. It was spotted by three vacationing California sisters who decided it was just what U.S. women needed.

Here's where the genius came in. Instead of relegating it to housewares departments or even to personal care departments (where it would compete with shavers, hair driers, and the like), they convinced department stores to position it as a beauty product sold in the cosmetics department.

Now, here's where a key consumer insight came in. Down through history, women have equated beauty with a bit of pain. Corsets, beauty regimens, hair removal, and dieting are mostly unpleasant experiences. The three sisters took the fear out of the machine and concept by telling consumers that yes, it would hurt—it would be unpleasant at first—but my, don't your legs look good?

But they did more. They camouflaged the pain and spent time and money teaching consumers the proper use of the machine. The product was demonstrated to women at the store level through personal contact and through glossy, high-production-value videos. Women were at first nervous, than intrigued, finally enraptured by the product and its benefits—no mess, no chance of cuts, and less frequent use.

The three sisters developed a share of heart for their product and ran all the way to the bank. They made so much money with the product that they were able to finance a big, brassy Broadway show!

Imagine if the Epilady sisters merely *described* the product instead of *showing the whole package* to consumers and retailers.

## Heart versus Mind

Physical product benefits and characteristics are only a part of the overall product picture. The emotional aspects of the product and positioning are just as important. When you fail to identify the product opportunity ahead of time in terms of the consumer's wants or needs (or don't learn about the emotions that will drive your product) you are merely guessing about your product's acceptance. Your product becomes a solution that's searching for a problem to solve.

It's also a truism that you and your people will get bored with the product and the emotion wrapped up in it long before the consumer does. Overintellectualization of your product is one of the deadly sins of marketing.

But when an emotional need has been fulfilled in a way that no one else has achieved, you have won share of heart, and you're on your way to a successful marketing opportunity. I learned how important this is while speaking with a young woman when I helped develop a new kid's toothpaste for Colgate-Palmolive. Actually, we didn't set out to develop a kid's toothpaste at all. We were looking to develop one based on taste or some other physical appeal.

The breakthrough came when this young woman looked at all our concepts and product ideas and said that they were meaningless and insignificant. This woman said that her friends, many of them unwed mothers, wanted reassurance that they were providing the best of care for their children. They wanted a product that spoke to these needs and to their children in a noncondescending way. So while we were exploring the world of physical tastes and textures there was a whole segment of consumers who wanted to feel good, to know that they were doing their job well. We extended the concept and found that most mothers had the same needs and desires. Out of this project came Colgate Jr. and a whole line of oral care products positioned to kids—and their moms.

*There's no such thing as a parity product*. The closer physically your product is to other products, the more you have to create a perceptual point of difference in the consumer's mind. The consumer takes cues from the price, the label, the smell, the brand name. The successful product offers the consumer an assortment of sensory cues and visual reinforcement. It can be a hybrid of creature comforts and good health.

Gold foil is now a prestigious cliché that works. Funky overwraps can also lend an aura to your product. The stimulating aroma of microwave popcorn is a natural sensation.

## How to Achieve Share of Heart

Here are some ways to achieve a share of heart. You'll find many more as you continue to explore your product with consumers.

### The Excitement of Discovery

Give consumers the joy of discovery. After establishing your key positioning, cook up new uses for your product. WD 40 is a household lubricant that was primarily purchased and used by men. Its marketers created a brand new sales base by targeting their advertising—in the media and on the container—to women. They even created a new "pocketbook size." By doing so, they took the mystery out of the "man's world" (perception, again) of household maintenance and made the product less intimidating.

### Do One Thing and Do It Well

You have to be careful not to claim too many benefits, however, especially in your advertising. Too many benefits tend to muddle up your message. A laundry list of claims, as opposed to saying you do one thing incredibly well, can actually dilute the product story and makes you lose credibility. Consumers invariably look for specialists. When advertising, emphasize *one* strong aspect of your product. More than that will confuse the consumer. Anacin's strong antiheadache claim is powerful and singular. It's so strong that even after the manufacturer took out one of its key ingredients, not one consumer complained.

### The Nurturing Experience

Bored and out-of-touch marketers say that the use of pets and kids in commercials and on packages is hackneyed and unoriginal. It probably is, but it works. And it always will. Show how your product can help make *someone else* feel better. Play up the nurturing aspect in all of us. The old favorite, Vick's VapoRub, and today's new Vaseline Nursery Jelly have a lot to do with the growing up experience. The smell, the textures, and the laying on of Mom's hands through the use of the product can all reinforce the nurturing experience. If the product is for young mothers, put a baby on the package. If you're selling a pet food, show a photo of Old Tabby.

Here's an additional hint. When showing a baby or puppy, or almost any kind of pet, always make sure that the eyes are wide, large, and opened. There's something about our genetic programming that makes big eyes effective and irresistible.

### Desire for Status and Achievement

We all want to feel special. Although we can't always get raves from the boss and reassuring hugs from our mates, we can all feel special to ourselves for buying and using a product. Self-deception isn't all bad. Give consumers a reason to feel special. This could even be achieved by a higher price or unique packaging. The credit card people have taken this to new heights as people segment themselves in castes in restaurants as to what color card they pull out of their wallets. Do you really think that people buy Mercedes's cars because of the engineering? It's strictly a rationalization.

### Perception of Pleasure, Desire to Be Stimulated

Have a little fun with your product. Adding a scent (providing you've developed a rationalization), a new color, or a new tactile sensation can help exploit the richness of the product positioning. The more emotionally involved a consumer gets, the more he or she will choose your product above all others. Indeed, a successful product appeals to as many senses as possible. That's why some coffee manufacturers spray a "fresh" coffee scent into their instant coffee. What could be more sensual than the name Caress on a bar of soap?

Ralston-Purina has learned that consumers want a little fun and variety when facing the daily chore of feeding the family pet. So they added a variety of interesting tastes and textures to their product and packaged them with colorful graphics and "smiling dogs."

### Take Something out of Your Product or Put Something In

Even if your product's recipe was derived from the hand-me-down recipe of your great aunt Ethel, it's not etched in stone. Adding and subtracting an ingredient can often make the difference between a success and a failure. Marketers across the United States spray vitamins on what is commonly called "junk food" to gain the good graces of General Mom.

## Let Consumers Know Your Product Works

The smell of bleach that lets us know that our clothes are clean. The scent of pine that shows us we did our cleaning job well. These are some of the positive reinforcements that show us that the product works. A mild mint flavor was used in Colgate Jr. toothpaste because that was the cue to moms that the product was effective.

A wall and floor cleaner without a strong or perhaps even obnoxious scent is usually considered ineffective by consumers because it doesn't reinforce the fact that the user has done the job correctly.

Don't just tell consumers that your product works. Prove it to them vividly, anytime they use it.

## The Desire to Belong

Create an affinity group. Americans are the "joiningest" people anywhere. If you don't believe it, look at how many clubs and affiliations are in your wallet. The credit card people took advantage of this by giving affinity groups their own credit cards.

Developing a club or group for kids is an excellent way to achieve trial. A midwestern bread bakery, Campbell-Taggart, hit paydirt when it developed Iron Kids Bread, bread targeted to children. Earthshaking, no. But incredibly effective. It was a white bread that promised all the nutrition of a wheat bread. But instead of preaching to parents and having them force-feed it to kids, Campbell-Taggart promoted directly to kids (as well as their moms). Lots of pictures of kids bicycling, and playing basketball and baseball. Sports programs for schools, communities—the works. The simple strategy was so strong, it helped propel the brand into third place in the nation.

One imperative to remember when developing a group: *Choose a group that people can aspire to.* For instance, if you're appealing to kids always show kids older than your target market.

## Take a Step Back from Your Product—You Might Not Know What You Have, or Don't Have

Joseph Coors was the president of Coors Brewing Company when Miller had developed the first successful light beer, Miller Lite. It was a super-hit and was changing the profile of the brewery industry. In order to drum up new business, Coors's advertising agency approached him to develop a new beer. They would call it Coors Light. Mr. Coors blanched at the thought and nearly threw everyone out of the conference room.

He said that Coors was the original light beer and that's why it had been a cult success on college campuses among students just cutting their "beer teeth." Although logically correct, Coors had misjudged what was happening to the beer market.

Although Coors was probably the guy they invented the word "irascible" about, he was a businessman first, and he reluctantly agreed to try a new Coors light. It was the highest-calorie light beer, but it quickly became an industry leader. Although the original Coors was lighter than other beers, it had never staked out its claim to lightness as had Miller. Miller had quickly preempted the light claim, and everybody, including Coors, had to play catch-up.

Interestingly, Miller wasn't the first to play the low-calorie game. A beer called Gablingers was launched in the late 1960s, but its low-calorie claim was considered too effeminate for real beer drinkers. It had no share of heart. Miller was the first light beer to show real athletes—people with whom beer drinkers could identify—quaffing the brew.

## About Business-to-Business Marketing

To the business community as well as in the consumer goods sector, products and their imagery are one. Share of heart is imperative in business-to-business marketing. Like consumers, business people are neither rational nor consistent in their purchase behavior.

It's up to you to develop the product that's fully consistent with the businessperson's desire to make money, grow, and be assured of a measure of security. And although the prospect talks about increasing business, there's a bigger desire operating here. To a business prospect, share of heart is helping him or her look good to management, get a promotion, or (more important) not to lose the job they have. It's important to cultivate an image of strength, state-of-the-art looks, and stability.

### Keep It Simple to Keep It Effective

In marketing, we tend to get too close to the product we manage or sell. We try to overcomplicate it and look past the simple solutions. We provide long-winded rationalizations for physical product benefits because we believe the consumer wants them. We're afraid that consumers will look past the blatant emotional sell. They won't.

A purchased product is a manifestation of how consumers want to feel about themselves, how they want others to see and react to them. It's up to the marketer to make everything about the product help the consumer achieve a positive self-image.

Unlike marketers, consumers don't theorize about what they want. They respond. Marketers define product benefits in terms of numerical scales. Consumers simply buy or don't buy your product.

## Summary

1. Give the consumer a vested emotional interest in the product you're selling and you have a winner in the marketplace. While marketers are selling from the mind, the consumer is usually buying from the heart.
2. You'll think your positioning or share of heart is too schmaltzy long before the consumer does. But the "warm fuzzies" a share of heart provides can lead to a long-term success.
3. The good taste or performance of the product can last 6 seconds or less, but the good feeling it provides can last a long, long time.

## Questions, Answers, and Additional Insights

*If my product does four times as many things as another product, shouldn't I brag about it?*
Usually, when a person has a need for a product, for instance, cleaning a window, that person reaches for the specialist in that job. It's much more expensive to create a need than to satisfy one that isn't there already. And it never makes sense to confuse the customer. Two years ago, Coors put the legend "Draft Beer" on its package. Sales slumped almost immediately as consumers became totally confused about what beer they were really buying.

*If competition is stronger than ever and the consumer is more sophisticated, isn't it more important to talk about tangible consumer benefits?*
That's why it's more important to talk about emotional benefits. In a parity environment and with tremendous competition, it's impera-

tive to differentiate your product in one way or another. A share of heart gives you the greatest opportunity to do this. Look how well the people who make frozen dinners have done. I've had this feeling that people really like airplane food. Maybe not the unrecognizable kind, but those with real chicken, pasta, and vegetables. With names like Healthy Choice, Le Menu, and Weight Watchers, marketers are really just repackaging the same food that's served on airlines and delivering a share of heart to consumers.

*I use the very best ingredients for my product. It's the very best out there, yet consumers seem to prefer the competition's product.*

It's too easy to get too close to your product. Sometimes, the best product is not the smartest. The word *best,* in fact, is a value judgment. A consumer's perception of what is good varies, as do what the consumer thinks a product is worth in terms of price and even when the product is used or consumed. For instance, a ballpark hot dog can taste a lot better than the identical hot dog made at home, even if the ballpark frank was made of inferior ingredients. You may, for instance, make the best coffee in the world, but if the consumer's standard of coffee has changed (which it has, thanks to the drip coffee makers), there might be only a small market for the real thing. That's why it's imperative to keep auditioning your product out in the real world of consumers.

# 5

# Market Research—Making Logic out of the Illogical

*Chapter preview:*

- ***The importance of basic market research***
- ***Basic research tools, techniques, and screening devices***
- ***How not to spend an arm and a leg***
- ***How is the product going to affect the consumer's life and will he or she really care***
- ***How to interview consumers***
- ***The importance of focus groups***
- ***Key scripts and tools***

Successful research can be boiled down to two words:

1. *Ask:* Ask the right questions to the right people.
2. *Stimulate:* Stimulate the right people to give up their secrets.

This chapter focuses on a systematic way of generating consumer reaction that you can believe in and build on.

Every person in the world has hundreds of needs. At any given moment only one or two are in the front of a person's mind. The other needs are latent, or unconscious. People consist of a wide range of continuous emotions. That's why categorizing them into numerical scales, like most traditional research, is misleading. Numbers can't capture something as complex and multilayered as a human being.

Research is the art of seeing things that are invisible. If you wait until the media picks up on the trends to capitalize on them, you often will be too late.

Comedians or entertainers who want to try out material don't ask people what kind of jokes they want to hear. They take the material on the road, in front of live audiences to get reaction. If audiences don't like a gag, the comedians dump the gag or change it. If it gets a fair response, they refine it. If the audience likes it, they keep it in the act and maybe fiddle or fine-tune it to make it better until it achieves the optimum reaction. Notice that our comics don't ask people if they would like to hear material about wives. They don't ask them to grade jokes or what are funny attributes to talk about. The comics deliver their lines and wait for the reaction.

That's essentially what our research program is all about: trial and error; the chance to try out all your ideas—everything that occupied your mind and kept you awake at 4 a.m.

It's ironic that the small companies who need well-thought-out, enlightening research the most don't think they can afford it, and companies that can afford it easily use it incorrectly. I firmly believe you're better off with no information than with the wrong information.

It's always vital to create a product that's in line with the consumer's existing mind set—*taking the path of least consumer resistance.* For instance, while reading this book, you're most likely going to take out of it what already jives with your preconceived notions. You're probably going to be skeptical about everything else. What you don't agree with, you're going to disallow. It works the same way with consumers too. But if they don't agree with *your* notions, they're going to ignore you and not buy your product.

A great many entrepreneurs hate research, and I don't blame them; 95 percent of most research in the new product area is wasted, ill-conceived, and self-serving. Even the word "research" is fraught with negative connotations. It's paper by the pound. It's impassive and gives the image of generating reams of paper for no other purpose than to generate reams of paper. Research is the opposite of the entrepreneurial mindset, and it doesn't generate cash flow. Entrepreneurs thrive on action, not academics, and most traditional research is academic.

The Workshop approach to research has only one purpose—to create a sure-fire new product based on real-world consumer motivation by learning what drives the consumer. Our research is applied research. The insights we generate are actionable immediately.

## The Key Scenario

The eight people drinking coffee on the other side of the one-way mirror may hold the key to your next marketing effort. These eight people, who may have no particular talent other than to breathe properly, may change the course of your business. You wince as the moderator sits down and shows them your ad or new product ideas. Will they like it? Or will they yawn? Welcome to our world of market research.

According to a consensus of business executives, the largest cause of product failure is *poor or misguided market research.* To err is human, to repeat the error is the bane of new products that are built on faulty insight, no insight at all, or outdated research.

Most research reports are obsolete almost the day after they are written. Most research is built on things that have happened already—it's historic. Six months later the information is as old and outdated as the 5-digit ZIP Code.

Another mistake is *overresearching a product* in the hopes that it will fail one obscure test or another so the sponsoring company won't have to take any risk at all by launching a product. Market research is the most abused tool in marketing today. Under-financed marketers think they can't afford it, and mega-marketers use it to screen out too many good ideas. Arrogant or just plain foolhardy marketers think they know more about their market than anyone else and don't need good research. That's why few marketers have more than one success. With so much slipshod and faulty research, is it any wonder that managers or entrepreneurs are continually baffled by the vagaries and idiosyncracies of human behavior and the marketplace? But it's those quirks in human behavior that will really make or break your product.

What is it about new products that makes the most conservative entrepreneurs forget proper business practices, lose their perspective, and, essentially, guess at success? Perhaps it is the initial discomfort of dealing with people you don't know and being rejected. Perhaps it's ego. But it's the unknown buying factors and insecurities that make *personal* market research incredibly important.

Delegating research to researchers (and I know some fabulous researchers) short-circuits the relationship between seller and buyer. Delegating research, or worse, using secondary data, must not be, although it usually is, a substitute for interacting with consumers. There is that human quotient and human inquisitiveness (if you don't have it, you shouldn't be developing new products) which can't be replaced.

Larger companies usually have a different problem—over-researching. They look for so many holes in their marketing program and in the product they're researching that they're bound to find some. Sometimes the research is so complicated that one misses the obvious product or positioning opportunity.

The basic assumption of much of new product research is fallacious. It's assumed that people have problems with currently available products. Researchers ask incisive questions such as, "Do you have problems with currently available products?" And consumers respond, "No, we don't have problems." The whole premise is wrong.

## Show Consumers What Can Be Done

Consumers don't spend their waking hours thinking of new products that will improve their lot in life. They simply react to what you put in front of them. Until someone invented the air conditioner, the refrigerator, or even the juice box, consumers were perfectly happy with what was currently available.

Existing products show consumers what has been done. You should be showing them what can be done, and how it may (or may not) improve their lives, so that they can decide if a new product will improve their lives enough for them to buy it. Actually, improving their lives is a bit too strong—you want to know if the product benefit will offer them enough incentive to exchange their money for it on a regular basis. The goal of all research is to stimulate consumers into telling you what they will buy.

You might want to look at research as if it were professional wrestling. Right, the semisport that pits Gorilla Maneater against Gorgeous Harry for the World-Wide Championship of the Free World. You can laugh and feel uppity, but professional wrestling is responsible for the largest pay-per-view grosses on cable TV, easily outgrossing such allegedly legitimate sports as the world heavyweight boxing championship.

Professional wrestling, in fact, can be subtitled "Market Research Made Simple." The criterion is simple. If the people in the audience aren't yelling, they're not having fun. It works like that in the new product arena too. You should try listening to the cheers and the boos. Most formal research in the new product area measures the cheers instead of listening to them. And if the manager or entrepreneur reads a report (which is almost always watered down in jargon) instead of taking a personal part in the exploration, the effect is even more diluted.

There are two major kinds of research: qualitative and quantitative. *Qualitative research* gauges the quality and the more personal and/or emotional aspects of consumer reaction. *Quantitative research* uses a much larger consumer base and tries to frame all answers in so-called predictive numbers. Our approach deals strictly with qualitative research, because like pro wrestling, we're interested in the cheers and the boos.

Insecure product managers and number crunchers claim qualitative research doesn't breed numbers—it's not projectable. MBAs tend to be numbers-crazed, because if they make a "no-go" decision, they have the crutch of something called "numerical norms" to fall back on. But they're wrong. Although you can't usually graph the results of your focus group on a computer, the emotions and insights you elicit can be projected among those of similar lifestyles.

A great deal of research is actually done to make sure new ideas fail. Really. A vice president of a major cosmetics firm told me he didn't care how many good ideas failed as long as he didn't back a bad one. His whole research department was actually set up to make sure products failed in preliminary studies so the company wouldn't have to invest in test markets—the elephant's graveyard of new product misses. No gain, but no pain.

A great deal of market research is based on the overwhelming negativity that all but rules out the breakthrough idea. It can be very disheartening to find out that the idea you love can't work because it didn't pass the Brand Hypercrest Study and it missed its norms by a 0.325 margin. How can you have a norm for a revolutionary new product when the product never existed?

As David Ogilvy says in *Ogilvy on Advertising* (Crown, 1983), marketing executives use research as a drunkard uses a lamppost, for support rather than illumination.

So what is the best kind of research? Our method works because it forces a potential customer (consumer or industrial) to make a value judgment about your product in front of you. It's vital that research be a hands-on operation. The hackneyed, much maligned form of consumer interaction called the "focus group" and the one-on-one interview are superb when used correctly. But few people know how to use them correctly.

A *focus group* is a gathering of people of similar demographics having a "focused" discussion about a subject, usually led by a moderator. I prefer to think of focus groups as consumer panels. A "one-on-one" is just what it says—one person talking to one other person about a product. The focus group transforms a dozen or so people into a microcosm of your target market. Focus groups and one-on-ones are the easiest and most economical ways to conduct market research.

It's amazing to me how many companies spend six jillion dollars on new product development and entrust their new product research to housewives or teenagers in a mall bearing clipboards. It's not that these people are bad people, but their goal is to fill in the blanks, not to get the right answer. Even if you acknowledge the plus or minus 5 percent error (as they say in the jargon), they're missing the thing that is going to make your research special: caring.

The following verbatim exchanges took place at a Westchester, New York, research facility:

After a clip from a movie was shown:

INTERVIEWER: "How funny did you think it was on a rating of 1 to 5?"

RESPONDENT: "Kind of funny, maybe a 3."

INTERVIEWER: "I thought it was funnier than that. Let's give it a 4."

RESPONDENT: "OK, whatever" (walks away).

After samples of a new ice cream were given:

INTERVIEWER: "Which ice cream sample did you like best?"

RESPONDENT: "None, they were all terrible."

INTERVIEWER: "But you have to choose one of the numbers on the sheet."

RESPONDENT: "But I didn't like any of them."

INTERVIEWER: "Okay, I'll circle number two, is that all right?"

RESPONDENT: "Sure."

Unless you're personally listening and watching the consumer's body language, you're missing a great deal of the consumer's real message.

Even a simple yes or no is fraught with meaning. For instance when an interviewer checks off the "probably would buy" box it could mean:

"I'm too polite to say no."

"If I had a coupon I might buy it."

"If I felt rich and carefree at the moment I might give it a shot."

"Yeah, fine—gotta get home for dinner, bye."

You and the clipboard-carrying researcher have different goals. You want to obtain consumer insights and honest opinions straight from the mouth of the consumer. The clipboard-carrying researcher wants to fill in a quota of boxes and go home for the night.

The structured fill-in-the blanks questionnaire also eliminates the serendipity factor—those off-the-cuff remarks that show how the consumer really feels. What appears to be a serendipitous remark is really a consumer's real-world reaction to a stimuli in a real-world situation.

## How to Research

At the risk of sounding like a half-baked graduate of Psych 101, there are two parts to basic research: the stimuli and the response. In this corner are the *stimuli*—your product, product prototype (if available), your concept boards, your new product team (all of them), and your probing questions. You can use a well-versed professional moderator as long as you're personally there to listen and as long as the moderator is flexible enough to make changes as you go along.

In the far corner are the respondents—the people you think might want to buy your product—who will give you the responses that will generate actionable insights.

## Concept Boards—Unlocking the Key to the Consumer's Mind

In the real world, consumers react to advertising, so create an ad around your product and ask probing questions. Create actual hand-drawn but full-color ads for your products (or services). These are known as *concept boards.* (See Fig. 5-1.) They should have the product, a headline with benefits, and selling copy.

Resist the urge to produce the white-card concept boards which have the outline of a product and maybe a line of copy. They're dumb. And boring. And too abstract for the consumer.

Show consumers the actual product (if available) with variations on advertising you'd like to do. Tell them the product is currently selling in Peoria (unless of course, you happen to be in Peoria). Would they buy the product if it was for sale in their area? Don't make the mistake of asking consumers to do your thinking for you. Because there should be a realistic illustration of your product on each of the boards, you don't have to create numerous real working products or expensive models at the beginning. As I mentioned previously, paper is cheaper than prototypes. You can create fifteen or so concepts with an unlimited variation of ideas for a fraction of the cost of one product prototype.

The goal is not only to find winning ads but to discern true purchase motivations in a real-world setting. Like in our ideation, we are interested in stretching the creative envelope and covering all polarities of your new product opportunity.

## Building on Rejection

When you talk to most people, they don't want to hurt your feelings. When doing market research, you want them to be brutally frank and honest. Better now than when the product is in the field. As hard as it can be, try to remember, they're attacking the idea, not you.

Rejection is an important part of consumer responses. We learn the reason for rejection and then mold negatives into positive concepts. Expect mistakes to happen. If rejection and mistakes don't occur, then you're not stretching the creative envelope to the limit.

Focus groups are easily the most popular form of research used today and with good reason. They're fast and relatively inexpensive at about $3000 per group. They can cost $1000 or less if you do your own moderating. Pioneered in the 1950s, focus groups were a prime mover of the motivational advertising revolution.

A focus group is an interactive gathering of people of similar backgrounds assembled to have a frank or "focused" discussion on a certain

**Figure 5-1.** New Products Workshop concepts: to consumers these are real-world products in real-world settings (pages 94 to 101).

**Figure 5-1.** (*Continued*)

**Figure 5-1.** (*Continued*)

**Figure 5-1.** (*Continued*)

**Figure 5-1.** (*Continued*)

**Figure 5-1.** (*Continued*)

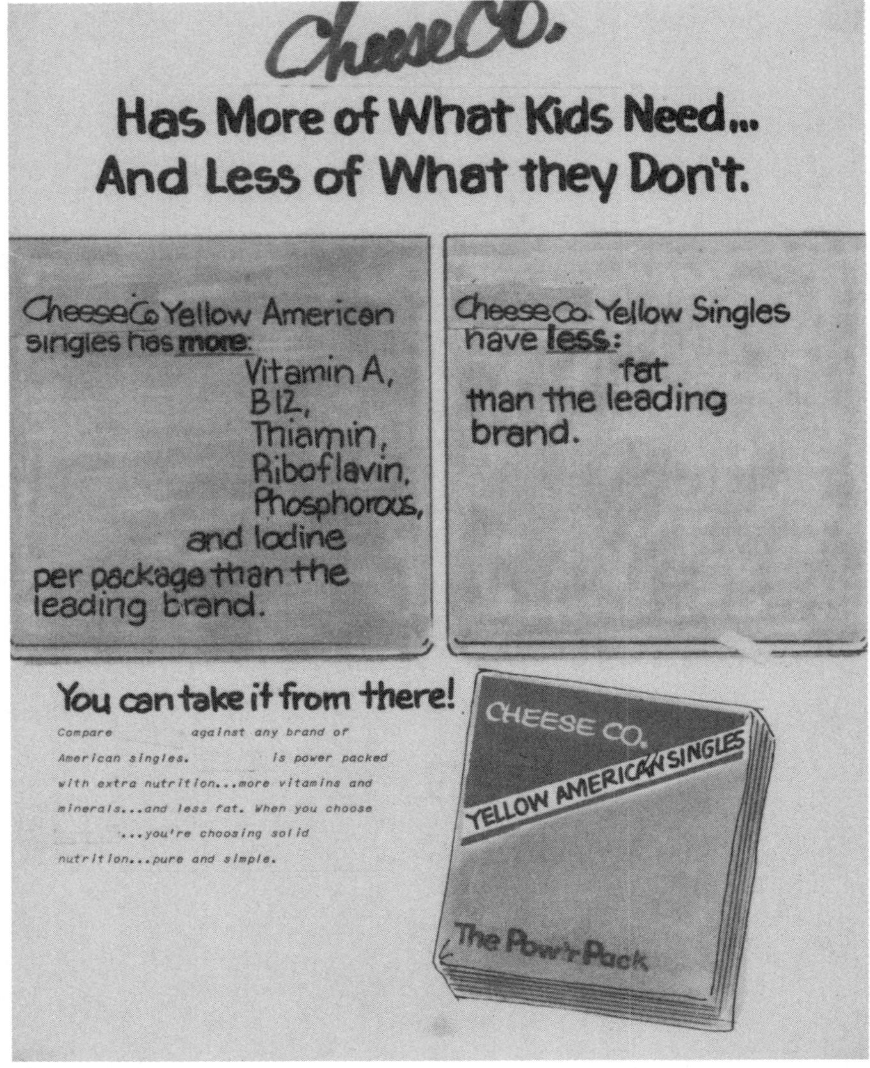


**Figure 5-1.** (*Continued*)

**Figure 5-1.** (*Continued*)

topic, product, or product category. They discuss how they use the product and what might have caused them to buy it. It's analogous to eavesdropping at a coffee klatsch or poker game and knowing you're the one that's being talked about. This small group of consumers are your eyes and ears to the real world. Optimally, a focus group is a data bank of the human mind and potential consumer behavior. Focus groups are being used and abused:

- A major health and beauty aids company ran over 65 focus groups as a first step in developing a new men's cologne and still considered the results inconclusive.
- Yet Colgate-Palmolive ran only nine groups over a three-month period to develop a mega brand, cut into their main competitor, and developed enough consumer insights to keep R&D busy for the next six years (I know, because they were my groups and my products).
- American Express used focus groups to boil down 250 new product ideas to 5 and created a department and profit center in a span of two weeks (my Workshop, again).

But are focus groups as useful in the 1990s? Is their value being surpassed by super-binary number-crunching computers and their MBA masters who can spit out demographics and psychographics in the same time it takes to read this paragraph? Are focus groups doomed to become the pet rocks of the electronic market research age due to overkill and misuse by slothful research managers? Or are they a vibrant marketing tool whose potential has yet to be tapped?

It all depends on how the focus groups are used and who's using them.

As often happens to the simplest ideas, something has gone awry in focus group land. Marketers are getting lazy and fearful, especially when there's a recession group-think mode. When marketers and advertising agencies have a shortfall of ideas and solutions, they expect consumers to do their homework for them. They expect focus groups to make decisions that they themselves used to make. Paula Singer, formerly market research manager at Shulton, Inc., Clifton, New Jersey, states the problem this way: "Managers are refusing to make decisions. They're using focus groups to make their decisions for them." When a marketing manager is unsure of a decision, the answer has become "Let's run more groups." Although this is good for the booming supplier business and research department, it doesn't say much for middle-management savvy. Dr. Neil Kalt, president of Artisan Research in Westport, Connecticut, and an experienced moderator, feels a focus group "is simply the best way to find out why consumers think and behave as they do." Kalt, who moderates in excess of one hundred groups per year, says, "You can get a pretty good feel for how a new product will do from the intensity of the responses that you see in focus groups."

## Questions to Ask

Here are some basic questions that should be asked in one-and-one research and in group interaction. These are meant only as a guide and should be added to as the need arises. Your own natural curiosity will manifest itself as more and more people talk about your product. At the end of this chapter is a complete suggested script for running your own focus group or research program. If you choose to moderate the group yourself, try to stay unbiased and be sure not to get offended.

*The product is a mythical frozen seafood dinner.*

*Category Behavior:* Respondents to detail their buying habits to find out how your products fit in with their lifestyle.

"What are some type of frozen or prepared dinners you buy?"

"How often do you buy them?"

"Where do you shop?" (The answers might give you an idea of the type of store that should stock your product.)

*Concept Comparisons:* Show concepts (ads) that you have created.

"I want to show you some ideas for a product. A company is looking for ideas and opinions about a new product (or products). These may look like ads, but they're really not, so I don't want you to say that the artwork isn't realistic or the people don't look good."

Show each concept one at a time.

"What is the main message of this idea?" (Makes sure your product is communicating what you want to communicate.)

"Who is this product for and why?" (It might be for kids, or husbands, or wives, or fulfill some, as yet, undiscovered need.)

"Why would the product be used? What would it replace?" (Assuming the weekly food budget is somewhat nonvariable, some other product will not be bought. This is a good way of helping you determine the product that might compete with yours in the consumer's mind.)

"On what occasions would you use it?"

"Where in the store would you find it?"

"Would it be in the refrigerated or frozen section?"

"How often would it be used?"

"How would it fit into your current lifestyle? Is this positioning unique? Is the product unique?"

"What would the product taste like?"

"What areas are negative or unclear?"

"Does the appeal motivate you enough to try the product?"

*Concept Comparison:* This is an open-ended appraisal/comparison of all the products. The goal will be to establish the ideal product (after locating the strongest concepts).

"Why are the favorites best liked? What sets them apart from the losers?"

"Are there any hidden benefits in the concepts?"

"Are there any common elements which can be used?"

"What refinements can be made?"

*Packaging*

"Which package do you think would stand out best in the store?"

"Would the sleeve package (assuming there is one) get you to try the product?"

"Which gives you the best expectations of the product?"

"If you could take the best elements from each package and build a new one, how would you do it?"

*Product Sampling (finally)*

"Do the products meet with your expectations?"

"Which concept best describes the product and might make you want to buy the product?"

"Would you buy the product? Which product would you buy?"

"Would you order this in a restaurant? Which restaurants? Which product?"

*Important note:* If the answer to the "Would you buy the product?" is conditioned by them having a coupon, or if there is no real emotion to the "yes, I would buy it," then your product is probably weak.

### Variants on the Procedure

Of course, you might not be working on a food product, but this method can be used in almost every business category with a little imagination and flexibility. For instance,

| If your product category is: | Possible stimuli might be: |
|---|---|
| Catalogs | Roughly drawn catalog pages |
| Magazines | Editorial pages, particularly potential covers |
| Impulse items | Roughly drawn point-of-sale displays |
| Business supplies | Different products to include in your inventory |
| Chicken products | Various types of new products that can be made with chicken |
| Financial products | Financial products with names, features, and, of course, putative benefits for these features |

### Who to Talk To

With a good facility (focus group facilities are located around the country) you can locate any mixture of potential customers and create a microcosm of your market in the focus room. Screening for possible respondents is a bit trial and error and a bit instinct, but here are some generalities:

1. Screen for people who buy a similar type of product on a regular basis. For instance, for the seafood dinner, you want people who buy seafood and prepared dinners.
2. Screen for people who buy your competitor's products. You'll get actionable information on your competitors' strengths and weaknesses.
3. Screen for people who buy regularly from the same distribution channel as your product, i.e., direct mail, home sales.
4. Screen for people who might have tried your product and didn't like it; screen for people who have tried your product and like it.
5. Don't screen for "creative consumers" or articulate consumers. Most consumers are neither articulate nor creative, so they're not indicative of the real world.

Figure 5-2 is an example of a type of screener that might be used for our mythical seafood dinner.

## Lick Your Wounds and Move On

All your questions can be asked and answered in two hours or less. If your product is national in scope, you must move into the diverse areas of the country because of regional biases and opinions.

When properly choreographed and run, focus groups reflect what your miniaturized society thinks and feels. When properly spaced over a variety of geographically dispersed locations, they accurately reflect how a cross-section of consumers will react to your concepts and products in the real world. Often a manager will book groups in a nearby area to save time and money and expect the findings to be projectionable nationwide. But it just doesn't work that way. Used correctly, focus groups allow companies to "test market" ideas on an extremely efficient basis and to learn a great deal about a category. It can be marketing's unique R&D department: building on ideas through trial and error.

There's no limit to how a focus group can be used when it's in creative hands. NatWest U.S.A., a major bank in England and the Northeast, used our focus groups to help introduce consumer mortgages to the New York real estate market. It competed against Citibank, a giant in New York banking, who was offering legal kickbacks to realtors. Also, because the real estate market was stagnant at the time, NatWest thought brokers would be tremendously rate-conscious.

NatWest hired us to develop marketing concepts, merchandising aids, and other incentive programs which were shown to groups of real estate brokers. We deleted and added new products and ideas as they were either accepted or rejected by the real estate brokers. The surprise findings were that NatWest needed to develop a program that emphasized service to brokers rather than the lowest rates or questionable rebates. In fact, the brokers at the groups had an almost emotional catharsis as they discussed how banks have continually let them down.

The important thing is to make adjustments as you go along. A great deal of misuse stems from a desire to control what consumers say and do. The unforeseen is becoming the unwanted. Everything must be buttoned down to prevent the unexpected—to make sure that no unplanned situation occurs that would make the manager look bad, which of course is the opposite of building on serendipitous events.

But controlling groups defeats the purpose of a consumer group. The reason that groups are so helpful is that there is give and take. Unfortunately clients expect a focus group to produce results that

New Products Workshop, Inc.

212-370-0980

521 Fifth Avenue, 17th Floor
New York, NY 10175

Sample Focus Group Screener

Client: ABC Seafood Supply Date of Groups: 4/11/92

Specs: Two groups, ten respondents each, of women, ages 21 plus, who eat frozen entrees or dinners, and seafood on regular basis. Should have range of incomes and ages.

1. Do you or does any member of your family work in any of the following fields: Marketing Research? Advertising? Any company that distributes or manufactures frozen foods? Yes___ No___ Yes, terminate.

2. Do you have any children currently living at home? Yes___ No___ (at least half should have children)

3. Which of the following categories best describes your total annual income before taxes? Under $15,000 (terminate) $20,000 - $39,000 ____ $30,000 - $39,000 ____ $40,000 - $49,000 ____ over $49,000 ____ (looking for a range of incomes)

4. Do you work outside your home? Yes_____ No _____ (at least half should have full or part-time jobs)

5. What is your correct age? _____ (seek a range of ages 25 - 55)

6. Do you buy a frozen dinner or frozen entree at least once every two weeks? What brands and types?______________________________

(Names include Swanson, Lean Cuisine, Le Menu, Oven Stuffers, and other local brands). If not, terminate.

7. Is this frozen dinner or entree for an adult in your home? Children? Both? ________________________ (at least 3/4 should respond adult or both)

8. Have you eaten any seafood, besides tuna, at home or in a restaurant in the past thirty days? Yes____ No____ (if no, terminate)

   What kind? ________________________ If not, terminate.

9. Do you or does any member of your family purchase and consume cheese on a regular basis? Yes____ No____ If no, terminate.

10. Are you currently on a strict diet to lose weight? Yes___ No___ If yes, terminate.

11. Are you currently within 40 lbs of your desired weight? Yes___ No___ If no, terminate

12. Have you ever participated in a group discussion for marketing purposes? Yes____ No____
    When was the last time?_______ (Must be at least six months)
    How many have you attended?
    Must have attended no more than three ever.

**Figure 5-2.** Screen for people who use your product and your competitors'.

match perfectly with the notions the clients bring in. Ideas and groups don't always work out the way you expect. The key is to be flexible and make adjustments. Negative feedback in a focus group is as important as positive feedback. Ideas that are discarded by consumers show companies possible pitfalls and prevent marketing pratfalls. They give companies the raw material of consumer viewpoints on which to structure a successful product or ad.

In developing our winning oral care products for Colgate-Palmolive, we exposed over 80 full-color concepts to consumers during a three-month period. At the conclusion of the assignment we wondered if working night and day on all those concepts was really necessary to create one product. We agreed it was. Every concept inspired a reaction of one kind or another which was built upon. The negative and positive concepts enabled us to create the product that avoided the mistakes of other entrants in the field.

## Don't Settle for Meaningless Head Nodding—Look for Raw Emotion

Marketers, particularly advertising agencies, often settle for what's called the "I'd buy it if I had a coupon" response. That's a major problem with focus groups. Management is told the groups were a success and consumers loved the idea. (Or, if they're still not sure, they say, "Let's run them through another set of groups.") But again, that defeats the idea of a group. The best response you can get is often nonverbal. Body language reactions that show real enthusiasm, words limited to the big three—"I'd buy that."

Moderators—the professionals who actually talk to the groups—speak of the frustrations involved in hearing the consumer respond a certain way and then having a manager (who failed to show up at the group) say it didn't happen that way. A rule of thumb is that if you didn't go to the groups you don't know what was actually said, or how it was meant. Although focus group facilities tape all dialogues, the tapes are rarely listened to.

The president of Dorman's Cheese Company, an East Coast manufacturer (now Dorman-Roth), sat in stunned disbelief as one group after another ripped cheese in general, his company's advertising, and his company. No report could have communicated what he learned by sitting in back of the one-way mirror (where companies see and hear what the consumers are saying "behind their back"). There was a happy ending though. He repackaged his product, renamed it, repositioned it in the market place (Deli Singles), actually increased his price, yet doubled his sales.

Even consumers, yes, consumers, are being replaced. They're being replaced by so-called consumer experts or "creative consumers." As virgin respondents are becoming harder to find, consumers are being used over and over. I know people who make a fair second income by attending groups. They're rapidly turning into a subclass of marketing experts. It's not only the facilities that are at fault on this point, it's the marketer who hires the facility.

It used to be enough to assemble a dozen or so users of a certain brand of soap. Now companies are screening consumers to be both creative and articulate. They're chosen because they supposedly have the ability to express in words why they want this particular brand of soap, as if they were going to write a thesis the next time they visit the supermarket. In the real world, consumers who are articulate and erudite are in the minority. They express their preferences in the only way that matters, which is by buying or not buying your product. Screening for creativity is misleading and not representative of the real world.

Why all this abuse of focus groups? To avoid the boring groups. To prevent the unexpected. Sometimes, because the truth hurts too much. Boring groups are part of the game. And so are sour groups. The fun starts when ennui is conquered by showing the consumer an idea or concept that makes them say "Aha! I want that product."

Dr. Kalt agrees that the intensity of consumer reaction that focus groups allow is a key part of the process. One insight gleaned from one stirring concept or question makes it all worthwhile. It's these insights into consumer reaction that allow marketing breakthroughs to be achieved. American Express's Gift Cheques, Union Carbide's Glad Lock Bags, Arm & Hammer's baking-soda-in-the-refrigerator concept all came alive because they stirred emotion in focus groups.

Ms. Singer, the former Cyanamid market research manager, states, "As marketers, we live in ivory towers. Consumer groups help bring us down to earth." Dr. Kalt adds, "If you want to find out how many, crunch numbers. If you want to find out whether or why, do groups."

## Ten Ways to Make Your Focus Group Imitate Real Life

The following are some good guidelines for running effective focus groups:

1. *Ignore the preconceived notion.* Keep an open mind. Stay flexible. The consumers are letting you in on their intimate likes and dislikes. Listen closely and react instead of getting defensive.

2. *Don't understimulate the respondents.* Signs of a bored group are easy to spot: glazed eyes, yawns, and requests for coffee, NO DOZ, or

their respondent's fee. Sure, you're paying respondents, but that doesn't mean you should bore them to death. Bored consumers don't want to admit they like anything, because then they're going to have to sit there and discuss it! It's easy to bring ennui to focus groups—by showing white-card concepts or those that have no relation to the real world or by using no concepts at all. Excite the consumers with real-world probes, products, and advertising. And then watch their eyes light up when they see something that turns them on.

3. *Don't give up on your concept or new product too quickly.* If consumers dislike an idea, don't drop it right away. Make changes and adapt to their opinions. A minor change in positioning or product form may be the difference between the success or failure of a product. Consumers buy physical product benefits and emotional benefits together. When you separate the two, your product will get shot down every time. Rejection of a pet product or ad hurts, but watching your rival come up with the same idea you let a focus group shoot down hurts more.

4. *Don't insist that your idea is good, whether consumers agree or not (the converse of rule 3).* Don't batter the consumers into submission. Try hard enough and they'll say anything you want them to say. Don't keep harping on the product idea until they're forced to say something good about it, then recommend a "go" to your company. "The consumers loved it. They wouldn't leave until we promised to mail them free samples." A product is good only when consumers insist they would buy it—without a coupon.

5. *Don't kill a product based on one set of groups or one location.* The United States is not a homogeneous collection of people with equal values, economic situations, and likes and dislikes. If the product doesn't play in New Jersey, it may play somewhere (or everywhere) else. Not everyone is going to like your concept. In fact, whole regions may take your concept, ad, or product as a personal affront. If at first you don't succeed, try, try again—but somewhere else.

6. *Don't overanalyze the results of a group.* (This one is committed mainly by MBAs, with some help from psych minors and bored researchers.) Don't analyze the results to death. Don't listen to the tapes over and over. Don't attach deep psychological meanings to everything: "Of course, the consumers raved over the product, but what do they know?" "They swore they would buy the product as soon as it was marketed. But does that mean they like it?" "How well will it graph?" When you show consumers something they like, you'll know. A simple, emotional response (yeah or nay) is a lot more valuable than a 125-page pseudopsychographical analysis.

7. *Don't ask consumers to read anything.* Reading is a very private matter. And a focus group, where people are meeting other people for the first time, can be a stressful, unnatural situation. It's virtually impossible to get consumers to comprehend anything about your idea if you make them read it. Read the concepts to consumers. Play show and tell, then let them react.

8. *Be there.* Encourage as many people as possible to attend the groups, otherwise they simply won't believe you, especially if your results go against their preset knowledge base. Attend the groups (and try to get everyone else to, instead of waiting for the book—the 125-page moderator's report that you requested but will never read). The most important parts of the focus group are the people behind the mirror.

9. *Eliminate* the two dreaded enemies of good ideas: the know-it-all respondent (who speaks "for the buying public") and the know-it-all marketer (who knows the buying public so well he or she translates everything the consumers are saying while they're saying it).

10. *Forget the midnight postmortem.* You've been sitting in a darkened room for six hours, trying to grasp more facts than the new IBM million-K computer can hold. Don't make a decision right now that will affect the whole life of the project. Resist all urges to recap. Go back to your hotel or home and sleep. Wait until the next day or so, and you'll be amazed how everything comes together.

Here is a recipe for actionable research: Get a good moderator, stimulate your groups well, and listen to the people you're trying to sell. Focus groups are more than a research tool—they're a marketing tool.

## Learning from the Whole Marketing Channel

Although it's important to learn about your market from the end user's point of view, it's also important to learn about who sells to the end user or who influences the sale. The influencers might have nothing to do with the ultimate, physical sale. They may be distributors, engineers, technical people—anyone in the sales chain.

For instance, if you were applying for a job, the last person you would want to speak with would be the personnel person, even though that person does the actual hiring. You would really want to find out the wants and needs of management and the people who would be the key influencers in the hiring decision.

In many projects, we spend a considerable time calling companies who have bought similar products and asking questions about who was active in the decision. More often than not, you'll find someone who is willing to talk to you.

### Moneysaving Alternatives to Focus Groups

Another way to get the information you need is to interview through one-on-one interviews. Most shopping malls have facilities that will buttonhole consumers for you to interview for about $750 per day or less. Have everyone in your group ask questions, on a one-to-one basis with consumers, and have the consumers compare ads. Try to get a wide open area so everyone can listen to each other's questions and answers.

## Summary

1. Research is when you can maximize your ideas for a minimum of money, make sure that you're right and that all avenues are thoroughly explored before you make large product expenditures.
2. The ideal research program has you and your new-product group interacting with objective groups of consumers.
3. In research, as in the entire new-product process, it is vital to stay flexible and make changes as you go along.
4. The key to research is to get consumers to react to what you put in front of them, not to intellectualize on what they think you want.
5. Full-color concepts are the ideal way to elicit response and to appropriately frame the consumers' reference points.

## Questions, Answers, and Additional Insights

*I've been told that focus groups findings are only about what one set of consumers feel about your product at any given time in any given area. Is that true?*

It's true. That's why you can't limit yourself to a specific area unless that's the area you plan on selling to. Research should be done in varying geographical areas among demographic groups representing your target populations.

*Why do I need all of these so-called stimuli? Why can't I ask consumers what their problems are?*
Because consumers don't always realize they have a problem unless you show them a solution. It never occurred to people that they might have underarm perspiration problems, until someone pointed out the problem...and the solution.

*I've been told that focus groups are not projectable.*
Although the results of a focus group probably can't be graphed on your Macintosh, feelings and emotions can be projected. It's sort of like a Broadway show that opens in New Haven. If it received raves there, you can be pretty sure that it will be received well on Broadway. If it bombed during tryouts, it will probably bomb in New York.

*I know the consumers didn't like my idea, but I feel in my gut they were wrong. Should I go ahead with the product anyway?*
It's your money, but even though my living is developing new products, I'll usually junk my opinion rather than the consumer's. I've been wrong before (I think); the consumer has a perfect track record. But you should try your idea in different positioning scenarios.

*How many concepts or prototypes can you show in a two-hour group?*
I have shown 30 or more concepts and gotten extremely constructive reactions and an unflagging interest level. The marketer tends to get bored long before the respondents do. However, if your concepts are dull or if you are ill-prepared, you are much more likely to experience consumer tune-out: If you're boring people in a controlled setting like a focus room, imagine the lack of interest that will be shown your product when—if—it hits the shelves.

*How many groups do you need for an actionable response?*
We find that six to nine groups or sessions of one-and-one interviews (two to three per geographical area) will generate more than enough information and insights to develop, optimize, and position the most complex product.

# 6
# The New-Product Development Process

*Chapter preview:*

- ***A holistic, proactive program that really works***
- ***Putting it all together from concept generation to the ultimate marketing road map***
- ***Eight key (and simple) steps to success***
- ***Creating a decision tree***

If you have read Chaps. 1 through 5, you now have the right tools and knowledge to create a successful new product. We can start changing the paper idea into something tangible. As you have seen, most of the factors for success actually occur on paper, before you start spending money on tooling up or on ingredients.

As an entrepreneur, and having worked with many smaller entrepreneurs and start-up companies, I know you are going to be impatient to develop the physical components of your product and take it out into the real world. When an individual calls me and asks for advice and I recommend spending on research instead of spending on advertising, the entrepreneur's face drops. I don't blame the entrepreneur. My face would drop too. Research does not usually generate funds. But rushing to failure doesn't generate funds either.

Early-stage testing in the actual market environment of your product allows you to validate or find flaws before the costly launch. Changing concepts on paper requires little more than a handful of markers and some tape. 'Tis a far, far better thing to make your mistakes now before you spend heavily on tooling and materials.

## Getting with the Program

So now it's time to put your new-products program together. This chapter is about developing a critical mass of consumer insights, creating a go/no-go decision tree, and acting upon it.

The following "protocol" is not offered without a little trepidation on my part. Any new-product strategy system can be little more than a "road map." A system can help you plan, can help you find directions, and can help you explore alternate strategies. But it is not a black box. It's not magic. You are the magician, however.

Our way to new-product development is a proactive, trial-and-error approach to winning the hearts and minds of consumers. It's holistic, because in the real world consumers don't separate the product imagery from the product itself. In the real world, it's the Gestalt, or the totality, of the product that provides the incentive to buy. Enthusiasm for your program should be built into each step. Ideas and new conclusions should be constantly added as you learn more about your market.

The Workshop approach spawns ideas and product premises the same way a laboratory develops products—by experimental trial and error. We're critical of accepted truths and hypothesize radical alternatives. In our approach, we modify preexisting ideas as we learn why consumers reject them and add new concepts as we gain new insights. In short, by developing ideas by evolutionary stages, we can spot a weak idea before it becomes a costly failure and can build a solid positioning concept that motivates consumers to prefer our product.

Indeed, because a product is more than the sum of its parts, all of our development is based on stimulating the consumer with a combination of the following:

- Product features
- Product benefits (a feature is useless unless it is coupled with a product benefit)
- Product personality
- Product image

Few knowledgeable entrepreneurs will approach a banker or venture capitalist without a complicated business plan that forecasts sales, growth trends, and other essential information, but few have a concrete structure for creating new products or a way of building on consumer insights on a disciplined basis.

In a highly structured company, the problem is totally reversed. The plan is usually so rigid that it becomes nearly impossible to develop a new product and successfully negotiate the twisty trails we talked about. Indeed, almost all new-products programs in a highly structured company rule out the touch of serendipity so necessary to create the breakthrough product.

In most companies it works this way:

1. Ideation
2. Fact finding
3. Elimination

(See Fig. 6-1.)

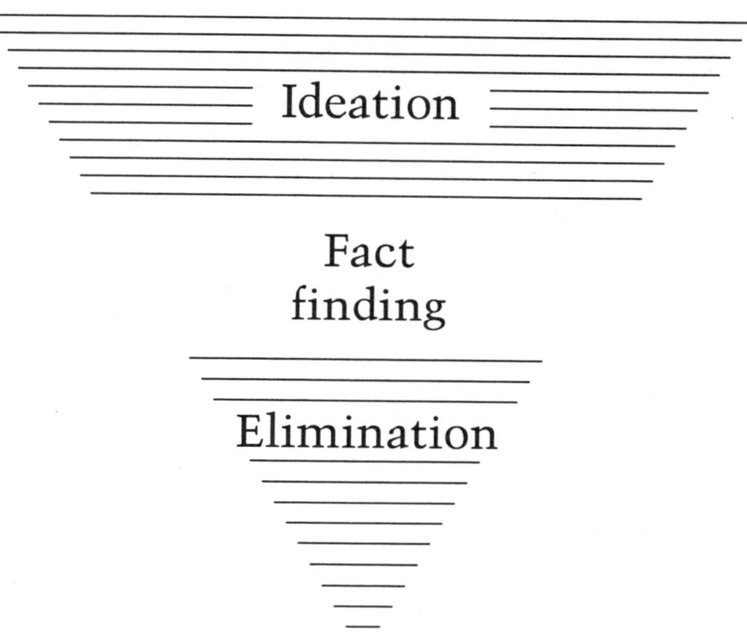


**Figure 6-1.** Traditional methods build on premises with a possibly faulty foundation. Figure 6-3 shows the better way.

Notice the key flaw in this strategy? If the idea isn't manifested in the original batch of ideas, it won't make the cut. If it fails because of lack of an *apparent* physical benefit, then there is no product. If you didn't position the product correctly the first time, you're liable to give up on the idea too quickly.

One reason most new-product work is conducted this way is simply because it looks good on a flow chart. It's easy to sell to management. It fits within most companies' existing (preconceived) work schemes. But despite razzle dazzle advertising and flashy annual reports, most products created by those big companies whose names are household words barely see the light of day. Who really decides which ones get thumbs up and which get thumbs down? The consumer.

That's why the Workshop approach builds on waves of consumer data, always changing, evolving to a winner rather than just eliminating products haphazardly. Admittedly, it's going to be hard to explain to management when you undertake an assignment that you're going to build a product on something you don't know about yet. But that's exactly what evolving from consumer insights is: learning and building on something you didn't know before.

Another fallacy is that there are two sides to every issue. There can be seven, eight, nine, or more. The purpose of building on insights is to gauge what's truly important to consumers and make sure that every variable is optimized, not compromised.

Bring R&D, engineering, and financial people together at the formative stages. Engineering a product is always going to be a compromise between job functions and departments. That's why we enlist our task force early. The goal is to foster a vested interest in the project as a whole, rather than its parts, among selected individuals. All ideas will evolve throughout the process. If you don't get the key disciplines together early, then resentment builds up and the NIH (Not Invented Here) syndrome takes place.

In the past several years the rivalry between R&D and marketing has gotten particularly out of hand. This has happened because R&D was used to developing the product and having marketing sell it. But as more products became available, there were fewer obvious consumer needs to be solved, so marketing has been forced to play a bigger role. R&D doesn't take kindly to this, especially being handed an edict from marketing. At the same time, though, R&D often can go off on a research tangent and forget that its goal is to make something that has to be sold to someone. That's why all disciplines must work hand-in-hand.

## Get Management Behind You

In a large company, the most crucial element of new-product development (almost always left out of marketing textbooks) is winning the hearts and minds of top management. The surest way to do this is to create products and product concepts that are demonstrably in sync with the company's consumer and technological equities. And you must do this without incurring the wrath of the various divisional egos and naysayers.

In a smaller company a different set of circumstances must be controlled. Although it's easy to say that the new-product group should meet regularly, meetings don't always take place when they should because others have different chores in the day-to-day running of a business.

In your new-product development program, managing people and changes is as important as managing budgets. Simply spending money on research and engineering, and only giving lip service to commitment, does not guarantee results. It's up to your task force, and you, to fully commit to developing a product that's fully consistent with the consumer's wants and desires and the overall strategic goals of your company; it's the manager's (or entrepreneur's) charge to make sure the project stays on track. Of course, it's silly to find a market or a consumer need for a product you can't make, but it's more foolish, and expensive, to spend money making a product that no one will buy. For instance, RCA's Selectavision was a well-designed machine, but who really cared?

## The Product Profile

That's why we develop the product concept and strategy statement early on—as your road map to success—based on consumer input. This is where you want to net out.

A sample product profile is shown in Fig. 6-2. Notice that the strategy

New Products Workshop, Inc.

212-370-0980

521 Fifth Avenue, 17th Floor
New York, NY 10175

SAMPLE PRODUCT PROFILE

Name: Deeep

Descriptor: Dry Formula, or semi-moist carpet cleaner

Key Positioning Strategy: A deep down clean that's so thorough you can feel it through and through. (It even cleans the soap scum that other products leave behind.)

Key Elements/Communications: Visual and all product descriptions communicate and reinforce deep down cleaning, i.e., the explanation is that the safe dry cleaning agent penetrates into individual fibers. Product should be lightly scented to reinforce cleaning proposition with sensory cue. Color of product should be white.

Packaging: Plastic bottle with pouring performance

Rationale/Appeal: Consumers are aware that shampoos and spray type products don't penetrate into carpet fibers. If they want to get a deep down clean they have to rent a machine or use a professional. The simple explanation gives a needed assurance to consumers that Deeep will penetrate and clean each fiber.

The "detergent residue" subhead is used two ways -- it provides reinforcement of the deep down cleaning headline, and attacks the residue problems of wet cleaners.

**Figure 6-2.** Sample product profile.

does not break the product down into its parts. Note also the absence of long-winded product descriptors and hyperbole and the lack of complexity. The strategy provides an ongoing checklist to make sure your product stays focused:

- Who is the product for?
- What will it do for the consumer?
- Why would the consumer want it?
- When would the product be used?
- Where can it be bought?
- How is it going to affect the consumer's life and positively relate to his or her lifestyle?

The competent researcher (or you, if you can't afford one) will provide the conduit for the task force. As we mentioned, the actual applied research is a hands-on function that should be carried out by all members of the team. Here's an example of a product built for all the wrong reasons:

**Slice of Life**

A manufacturer of marine sonar devices was requested by its sales force to develop a limited range LORAN (a radio homing device) for weekend boaters. Although built by a leading (and prestigious) manufacturer, the product was to carry a low end price tag. The thought was that weekend boaters really didn't need the extra range and would be unwilling to pay a lot for it.

Logical, right? The product failed dismally. The postmortem revealed a startling fact. Weekend boaters don't like to be considered weekend boaters. They have invested a great deal of time and money in their boating interest and want to be thought of as knowledgeable and adventurous. They want to feel like they could be the second coming of Magellan, even if they never take their boat out of the harbor. A higher price would have played to this feeling.

Group research or even just showing the preliminary concept to boaters would have flagged down this fatal flaw. It's far more expensive to create a consumer need than to exploit an existing one or to fix up mistakes once they've been executed on the production line. Isn't hindsight wonderful?

## Defining Your Objectives

Here are the questions you must answer before you spend heavy-duty money tooling up or physically implementing your grandiose plan. All these answers should be written down in some sort of coherent form. I know that many entrepreneurial types like to keep this kind of data in their head (me included), but writing a coherent synopsis forces you to clearly outline your thoughts. Although the mind can play tricks with ideas, writing forces the new-product developer to think, look, ponder, and review more thoroughly and less abstractly because the ideas are in cold black and white. The document will also help you sell your idea through the company, to investors, and/or to potential acquirers. The document is not written in stone—more like butter. Changes will constantly be made, and the document becomes even more important as the project evolves.

*Size of Market*

How big a market is the product in dollar volume? Is it really going to be worth your while?

How can you expect your competitors to react? Be realistic, even a bit on the negative side (pretend your competitors know as much as you do, but don't show them this book).

*Key Product Benefits*

What is the key product benefit?

Can its appeal be instantly communicated via mass media, at the point of sale, or on the package?

What are the user expectations—both sensory and in terms of performance?

What sensory cue will be expected by the consumer to reinforce the basic product and positioning?

What sizes will be best received?

*Brand Names, Packaging, Delivery Systems*

What are the optimum names and packaging configurations needed to drive the product?

How can the convenience aspect of the product be rationalized by the consumer?

What is the ideal packaging configuration? What are the label requisites?

Can leveraging an existing brand name inspire trial and purchase?

What stores should be targeted?

*Target Market*

Who is the target consumer?

When is the product expected to be used?

What current product will be replaced?

What is the main benefit to the user?

What is the emotional appeal?

*Key Communication*

What are the key communication elements necessary to support the product?

## Getting the Answers Through Insight Evolution

Although this seems like a lot of information for one project, it's not only basic—but it's also the end product of the research methods we've discussed. *Insight evolution* or *pyramiding* is the building of insights through sequences of consumer dialogue, until the most important insights are used to generate end user enthusiasm for your product. (See Fig. 6-3.)

These are the steps in developing the product. By following the suggested time frames, you can make sure your program is continually charging ahead and that your task force's enthusiasm is not replaced by ennui.

1. *Initiate a group discussion, initial ideation, and general orientation with your project team, including key members of R&D, engineering, and research.* You can also include possible vendors and your advertising agency. Ideally all members of the team should remain on the project until the end. Discussions should include long- and short-range goals, initial product directions, and advertising. There should also be an overview of technical capabilities, marketing, and sales channels and capabilities.

Time frame—about one day.

2. *Develop an inventory of hypothetical product superiority benefits.* The objective is to make a starter list of possible product superiority objectives by guessing at hypothetical consumer problems you can solve. These can come from your brainstorming sessions, your advertising agency, or outside specialists. These can also come from suggestion boxes or your complaint letter file. These will be added to, modified, and refined through the course of your project. Existing products and prototypes can also be included in this listing.

Estimated time—one week.

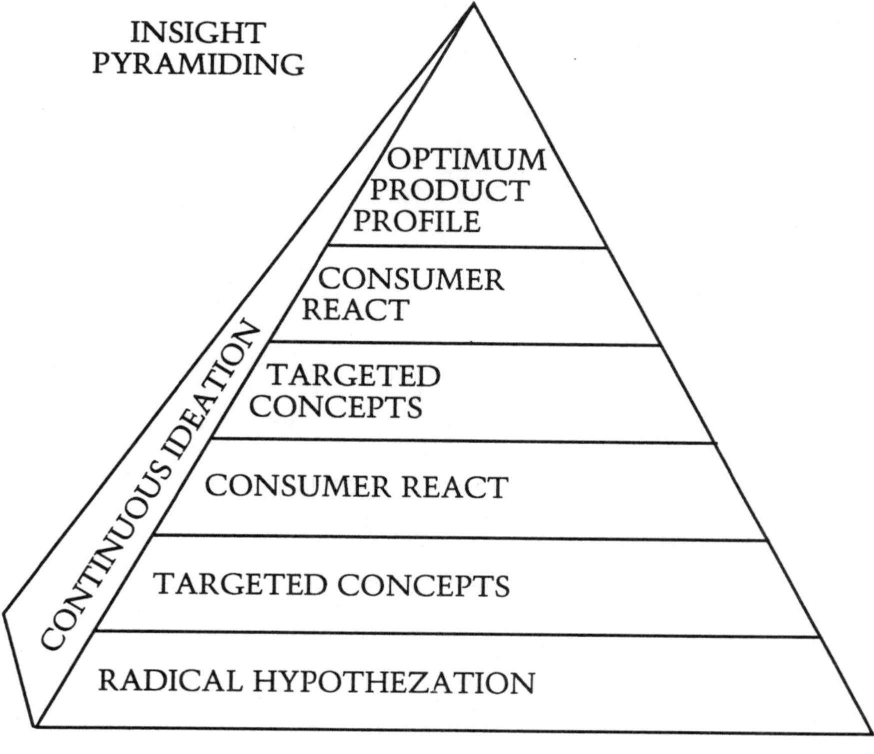


**Figure 6-3.** Building on insights means evolving your product based on learning about what drives your category here and now.

3. *Develop realistic concepts.* The best of these concepts (a judgment call, at least initially) should be converted into rough advertising layouts, complete with packaging, product benefits, and, of course, the product. You can also render existing competitive products in the same form to make sure yours is the better performer. Each of these concept boards should read like a mini-ad.

As we've noted, the concept board is the ideal way to experiment with ideas and to give each of the departments or members of your task force the freedom to test their own personal biases and ideas. Each department should have the freedom to develop its own concepts. You can help them in getting their concepts produced.

Resist the consumer diversion called the white-card concept board, which merely states product benefits or features. It's horribly misleading because it doesn't represent anything tangible or emotional to the consumer. Also, resist the urge to limit the number of concepts to an arbitrary number. The number of promising ideas will be whittled down, all too soon, by the consumer. If you already have a product, you *should* develop concepts exploring positioning, advertising strategies, and pricing issues.

Estimated time—one to two weeks.

4. *Evolve your concepts through consumer reactions.* Using the concept boards as your stimuli, your research maven (or you) should initiate a series of brief one-on-one interviews with consumers to get a preliminary overview of your market. (Note to novice marketers: Any library should have a list of research facilities that can help you acquire respondents.) All members of the task force should interview consumers armed only with the concept boards and note pads. Each of the interviewers is (or should be) a professional, and natural inquisitiveness will provide the raw materials for questioning. Any uneasiness will be gone by the second or third consumer interview.

The next step is to expose the concepts to interactive focus groups among people who represent your potential target consumers. At least one group should consist of regular users of your competitor's product, in hopes of finding an exploitable weakness. The objective is to gain new and actionable insights into consumer attitudes, to uncover triggers to consumer purchase. An open mind and elephant-thick skin will aid you as consumers poke holes in your pet ideas. If you're working in a business-to-business situation, probe everyone involved in the purchase decision.

Estimated time for first set of groups—one week.

5. *Build your product from insights and create a decision tree.* After the one-on-ones and after each group, concepts should be added to,

deleted, and modified on the basis of consumer reaction. Reaction to the concepts should be strong enough (even negative enough) to give you ammunition to make a go, a no-go, or a modify decision about each concept or product. The process continues until the most prominent consumer motivations are identified, positionings are realized, and the actionable product configuration is defined.

Prototype models and products should be developed from the most promising concepts. Since your goal is always to develop *actionable* insights, these prototypes should be shared with consumers to make sure you are delivering on the concept. If you already have your product, then it too should be shown to consumers to make sure you're delivering what they expect.

At the project conclusion, the concepts will have gone through a comprehensive set of consumer tests to confirm their validity, their communications value, and their impact. Moreover, the product will have been developed from expressed consumer needs and tested to make sure those needs have been well met.

Estimated total project time—about three to four months.

A typical project will take three to four rounds of focus groups, each round consisting of two or three groups spaced approximately three weeks apart. A broad assignment—say, finding a new surface cleaner—will require more groups and more concepts than a more finely defined assignment such as developing a furniture cleaner.

Time can be cut by as much as two-thirds by concentrating energies and resources into a more concentrated timespan.

## Let Consumer Segments and Benefits Drive Your Product

Let's assume you now have the big idea, the next major consumer hit. If you did your concept homework well enough, you have developed your product concepts as realistically as possible and therefore know what features the product should have and what the necessary cues to consumer performance are.

If you were really persuasive, your superiors, potential backers, and bankers have sat in on selected focus groups and have been overwhelmed with the consumer reaction. They might have even interviewed consumers in the one-on-one phase.

You have now enlisted the love and support of your task force (well, the support, anyway) and decided that the new-product investment is in sync with the wants and desires of your company. Of course, you know your competition's strengths and weaknesses and know how to exploit the weaknesses.

## Making the Product

*Now, all you have to do is make the product.* Once you feel you have the go-ahead, it's time for the transformation—changing your "paper" idea into a physical product. The actual physical development can be handled by you, but it's usually left to your vendors, engineers, designers, draftsmen and other technicians. But even if you are not personally involved in direct manufacturing, this is not the time to drop from the scene, as often happens in multitiered companies. These design and engineering groups should have been involved in the information gathering from the very beginning, going over design alternatives which have been presented to the consumer. You should be making sure that the product is created the way the consumer wanted it.

### Keep It Simple

An overengineered product is as much to be avoided as an underengineered product. Complexity breeds complications. Unfortunately, the tendency is to add a new bell and whistle at each step of the management approval process. But when you do that, you make the product more complicated to manufacture and more complex and expensive for the consumer.

Simplicity and ease of use and manufacturing should be a single-minded goal. Although engineers and product development types love complicated solutions to problems, consumers don't care. A needless complexity will reap havoc when a consumer finds it's just another thing that doesn't work.

It is often best to hold complicated trim and value-added items until a product enters a more advanced stage and consumers are willing to pay more for them. Put them into the drawer until you need them. And you will, as soon as the competition finds out what you have wrought.

### Don't Improve Your Product to Death

An undeniable part of the psychology of product development and engineering is that the more you and your task force (and management) look at your product, the more you'll find the idea simplistic, obvious, and boring—especially if the product is based on an emotional foundation. But the consumer won't think so. Resist the urge to make constant, unnecessary changes that add to the manufacturing cost. Changes should be done in the concept and prototype stages. Every change should be validated by your end user before you rush into it.

Keep running additional reality checks by returning to new consumer groups as new prototypes are developed. This, as well as constant reviews of your strategy statement, will make sure that you stay tracked and don't shoot past the consumer mark with unwanted changes.

Many new products seem to betray common sense. For example, although almost every consumer will praise all-natural and quality ingredients, in the real world the consumer won't always pay for them.

### Make or Buy

Transforming the concept into a product is largely the result of merging the desires of the consumer with the actualities of business life. The intricacies and complexities of building your product are largely beyond the scope of this book, but I can offer these generalities.

The key variables are cost, quality, and speed. You must assume your competition is already trying to fulfill similar needs (not as well or efficiently, of course). With a completely new product, you are undoubtedly considering the use of technology that is markedly different from that which you currently use. Unless the product is simple to manufacture, you will surely find it necessary and more economical to purchase existing technology from outside sources. In general, unless you can make the product with your current machinery with a minimum of modification, you should purchase the technology.

Resist the urge to force-feed your current technology into new applications just because you can do it. It's false economy, because you may be tying up the very machines that have created the product that is currently paying your salary. Later, when the new product has been launched and has a somewhat predictable track record, the technology can be brought inside.

However, your machinery may be fully operational, and may be modified to keep your product inside. Or you may have launched the new product project to alleviate downtime and keep your machinery busy. It can be quicker and, of course, easier to coordinate an in-house project, since fewer people are involved. A good operations manager (who, naturally, has been involved in your program from the beginning) should be your best guide.

When buying from the outside you will be dealing very closely with vendors who should be considered partners in your venture. They will help you fine-tune your preliminary model and will subcontract for technology and resources they might not have. Although the majority of vendors are extremely scrupulous, have signed confidentiality agreements close at hand. Once an opportunity has been identified, vendors should attend consumer groups and have access to your end-user research.

*A moneysaving tip:* Moderating consumer groups is often handled by professional moderators. Your local research facility undoubtedly has a list of professional moderators. But you can learn to do it yourself, providing that you can emotionally divorce yourself from the products. You can adapt the questioning techniques mentioned in the last chapter to your specific needs.

### Financial Projections

Here's where book work is in order. Here are the financial questions you need to answer:

- What are the annual industry sales?
- What share can you reasonably expect immediately? In a year?
- In five years?
- What volume can you expect?

### The Competition

Don't forget to assess the competition. You'll be surprised by who they are and what they might do. You should know at all times what kind of market activity you may be stirring up. Many entrepreneurs look across the new product sea and spot no activity, but you can be sure that other marketers are gearing up their profit boats. Peoples Express, when it ruffled American Airlines' feathers, should have known there would be a price war when it tried to enlarge its market and that there was no way it could win.

It can even be hard to figure out who the competition is. For instance, in my business, major competition is not the large new-product shops, think tanks, or advertising agencies, but the little guy who just got fired from his managerial job, bought a $9 batch of business cards, and set himself up as a consultant.

In any business, the market is always moving, ever evolving. It is impossible to successfully compete and isolate yourself from worldwide changes in markets. Often the respondents in consumer groups know what's going on in their markets before the trade press.

Your competition will keep you alert. Whatever new product road you take, you should probably assume that the competition is (almost) as smart as you. That's why a successful new-product program is continuous, and seamless, going from one opportunity to another.

## Summary

1. Although luck does play a part in new product success and one should never downplay the part of merely being in the right place at the right time, the odds are improved vastly by paying attention to these early steps and exploring all sides of the selling issues. These stages are:
   - Define your objectives
   - Put your team together
   - Develop hypothetical alternatives (radical hypothezation)
   - Consumer feedback
   - Evolve, add, and delete
   - Verify findings
   - To market
2. One of the most important steps in getting new product approvals for launching a product in a large company is to make sure your product is demonstrably in sync with your company's assets and capabilities.
3. Until your product is established, it usually makes sense to buy the technology from the outside, rather than having your own machinery tied up.

## Questions, Answers, and Additional Insights

*C'mon, is this the only way to develop a new product?*
There are many alleged systems for developing new products, but none can guarantee success. This program is undoubtedly the safest and the surest. It has evolved from a methodology that has proven itself for over two decades. The penalties for skipping a step include the potential for missing a key opportunity or making a serious and expensive misjudgment of omission or commission. Even the most advanced designed product—an epitome of workmanship and fea-

tures—won't help the company who develops a product for which there is no market or who lacks the means to create one.

*How efficient is this in business-to-business marketing? How can you get business people in the same focus group room?*
This approach is excellent for business-to-business marketing. You can often get excellent cooperation and generate key insights needed to develop a product that fits directly into your prospect's business plan. Although sometimes it can be difficult to get certain business specialists in a room, most research facilities have broad experience in obtaining hard-to-get respondents. But you're not limited to research facilities. You can bring your concept boards and prototypes directly to your prospect's place of business. Executives are often glad to help, often due to simple inquisitiveness. Just assure them that you're not going to try to sell them anything... yet. People love to talk about their businesses and sound smart.

*At what stage should the consumer be brought into the process of product development?*
Although the consumer is the beginning and end of the new-product development process, it's best to talk when you have your goals thought out and your concepts and hypotheses ready. The goal is always to get the consumer to *react* to what you are doing.

*But I sell a service, rather than a product.*
A service should always be considered a product. And a product should always be considered a service.

# 7
# Distribution Systems and Selling It In

*Chapter preview:*

- ***The vital importance of constantly selling***
- ***How to rally your new product team (and management) behind you***
- ***Selling to the trade***
- ***Establishing distributor relations***
- ***Taming the heinous "slotting allowance" monster***
- ***Traditional, new, and unconventional distribution avenues***
- ***Selling through direct marketing and those new-fangled, irritating infomercials***
- ***Finding the distribution system of least resistance***

Every entrepreneur and every new-product manager is going to learn this quickly: Coming up with the idea is simple—even producing it is a snap—compared with selling it. Despite the cliché that says "build a better mousetrap...," first you'll have to sell the mousetrap to:

- Your task force
- R&D
- Your management
- Your president

And that's only the beginning. Then you'll have to sell it to:

- Your sales force, who must sell it to
- The distributors, who must sell it to
- Their store clients, who must sell it to
- Their salespeople, who must sell it to
- The consumer, who may or may not have a mouse problem!

(See Fig. 7-1.)

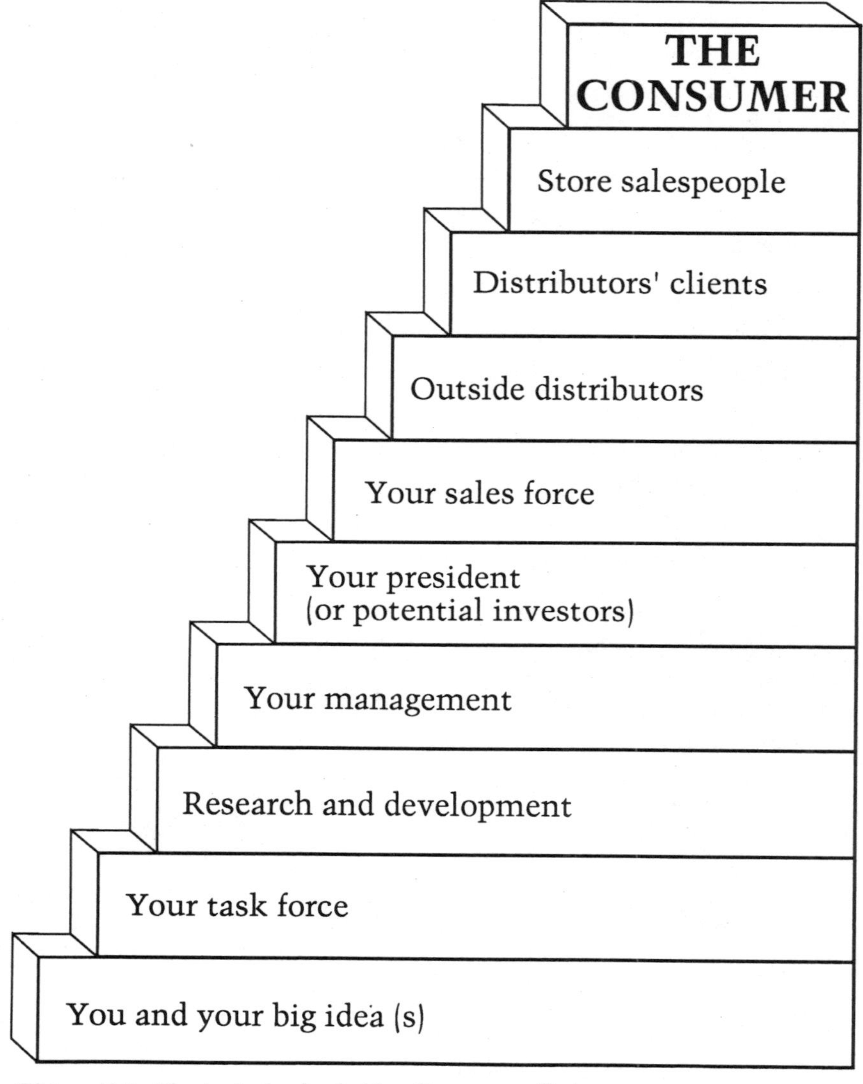


**Figure 7-1.** The typical sales ladder. Everyone sells to everyone.

This chapter is about selling it in and the necessity for being a salesperson. Yes, I know the word *salesperson* has a negative connotation, especially if you graduated from some fancy MBA school. The word *marketer* is much preferred, but whatever you choose to call it, it doesn't change the facts—when you're not selling, you're not making money.

This chapter is also about various distribution systems and how to take advantage of alternative channels if traditional systems don't fit your needs or if you find them lacking. A distribution system is the entire network of people who get the product from your factory or warehouse to the ultimate consumer.

Selling is the engine that makes your new-product program move. Few products can move themselves without a healthy dose of selling on your part. As we've said many times, all new products start and end with the consumer buying something. But consumers don't buy until someone gives them the opportunity to buy.

There are two major kinds of selling for the new-products person. Intercompany—selling within your management structure—and intracompany—selling to other companies, stores, and the like.

We tend to overlook the intercompany sell, but it's just as important as selling externally, especially if you're working in a tiered marketing environment. Anybody can, and often will, break your program if you let them. As you know, some people never grow up, and petty jealousies remain.

It's a sad fact of corporate life that people are more concerned with how they look to their peers and management than with what they can accomplish. The best defense against this attitude is a strong offense.

That's why it's of supreme importance to make sure that everyone, from your immediate superiors up to the president, recognizes the importance of your new-product program. Management must do more than just give you financial aid and lip service. It must stand behind you fully. It must also give you the authority to ask various support departments and even competing divisions for their cooperation and help. From my experience, more good ideas are killed off by divisional squabbling and politicking than by the consumer. One major financial company, now hurting, shot down at least five breakthrough ideas that its major competitors eventually developed on their own because the ideas weren't generated by the proper division. The success of your program depends on common goals. If there is divisiveness between departments and divisions, the program simply won't work.

Of course, every person in every department in every division in every company has her or his little quirks. You have to know your people. Some people will shoot down an idea immediately, but the next day, after the idea germinates, they'll come back and try to sell you on it, as if they had thought of it. That's the one thing common to all new-product development programs. If the product is a hit, everyone from the busboy who clears the table in the company cafeteria to the account executive at your advertising agency will claim credit. If the product fails, no problem—your fault.

Here are some do's and don'ts for selling your program and product to management:

*Do* sell the dream, and explain fully, what's in it for the company. "Tease" management with examples of success, facts, figures, and the results of your consumer work. Give credit to everybody who's been working with you.

*Don't* overdo the meeting bit. Every unnecessary meeting gives someone an opportunity to shoot down what you're doing. Two rules of thumb—if you don't have to have a meeting, don't. If you can't get something concrete out of a meeting, then it is a waste of time. Always have a purpose.

*Do* develop a "slim" briefing on what you're doing with the hows and whys of how you're doing it.

*Don't* hide rationalizations for your programs behind 500-page reports. Nobody cares. No one will read it. Nothing camouflages a paucity of ideas better than reams of paper. Resist the urge to do dog-and-pony shows for your own management. It's an abhorrent waste of time and money. (Dog-and-pony shows can be super, however, for sales meetings and intracompany sales.)

*Do* show progress—always. Show them where you've been, how you got there, where you're going.

*Don't* worry about persuading the negative thinkers. You know who they are. You'll never sway them. Ignore them, and hope they'll go away.

*Do* elucidate next steps and give management an opportunity to react.

*Don't* let things hang. Inertia breeds inertia.

*Do* tell the whole story or show the whole picture.

*Don't* give part of the story or half of your presentation. Wait until you can share the whole story and *show* people you gave the problem the proper thought time. Several years ago I worked at another new-product development firm. Often, when the president asked me for an opinion or recommendation, I gave him the answer within seconds. He would invariably glare at me and mumble something about me shooting from the hip. But I learned. In the future, I said "I'll work on it overnight and get back to you tomorrow." When the next day rolled around, I gave him my answer and a full explanation of my thought processes (which he always appropriated as his own when he spoke to the clients). He always went with my recommendations when I learned this little trick.

## Three Vital Tools for the Entrepreneur

If you're an entrepreneur, you don't have the headaches of the corporate world. Instead of having to sell to the company and "everyone else," you just have to sell "everyone else."

Three valuable things you own are your brain, your telephone, and your typewriter (or computer). They're all used to build a continuing and actionable contact list. Almost everyone you meet in the course of doing business should be a contact and hopefully lead you to an additional contact. Trade shows, of course, are a great source of contacts. So are secretaries, salespeople, and receptionists. Often they're superbly knowledgeable and can be quite willing to help you with personnel comings and goings. Never underestimate the power of a secretary. Secretaries can help you make the important distribution contacts, or they can blow you off with a simple "She's not in." Chapter 11 offers some tips on getting past the gatekeeper/secretary.

## Research Your Distribution Avenues Fully

It's vital that you learn the ins and outs of the available distribution systems for your individual category. Some industries use independent distributors. In others the contact is directly to the stores. Some industries offer a combination of the two. You can find out how your distribution system works by tracing it backward. Start with the final point of sale (for instance, the retail store) and ask the merchant how the product got there. If it came from a distributor, call the distributor to find out how it learned about it.

Trade relations are often neglected or minimized. The trade, of course, is usually your first customer. The trade can often control your product's future. You should research your prototype or product concept with the trade prior to your introduction to determine what kind of programs will be expected to get your product introduced into the store. Answers to trade issues can provide you with the information necessary for the development of a more efficient marketing program and rally trade support behind you.

Selling to the trade (usually a distributor, store, or chain) is similar to selling to the management of a corporation. Successful presenters follow these guidelines:

- Tease for action with success stories
- Talk about the distributor's interest, not your own

- Sell the dream, but tinge it with reality
- Sell the entire package or program
- Anticipate questions and stimulate the potential purchaser to react
- Spend most of your presentation time questioning and listening

To be a bit abstract, you're not really selling a product to the distributor or store. Your product can be thought of as a tool that will enable distributors to accomplish their goal of earning more money or building a better business.

Williston (Bud) Holbert, top sales trainer and president of Executive Resources in Plymouth, Massachusetts, stresses the importance of listening and questioning rather than selling: "When you question prospects nonthreateningly, they will often tell you everything you need to know to make your sale and will often outline their own dream." (After your probing questions) "you just have to fit your product with their dream."

Sometimes the dream can be totally unrelated to making immediate profits. When we shared our medical product concept that we developed with its eventual manufacturer, we spoke about revitalizing his company with new product categories. His company wasn't in medical products at the time. We also talked of fighting off low-cost foreign imports with a new patent for the product. (The patent's still pending, so I can't disclose more details.) To us, he presented the dream of working with a stable, long-established company.

It's also important that all interchange occurs in a positive environment. If you're under a time gun and can't tell the complete story, it's usually wiser to set up a new date. Also, if the key people can't be there or if a key decision maker cancels out, then it's best to postpone your meeting. Nobody can tell your story as well and as completely as you can. If you've made a presentation and are told "We'll discuss it with the boss," try to be present at the follow up meeting. Say something like "We've gone over a great deal of material today. Research shows that 90 percent of what we learn is forgotten almost immediately. We'd like to come back and meet your boss. When can we set something up?"

Try it. It can't hurt. You often get only one shot, so make sure you get all you can out of it.

You and your salespeople should be thoroughly armed with sales ammunition for all presentations and meetings. Be ready to capture a prospect's attention with dramatic tales of success. One of my clients, a manufacturer of prepared seafood entrees, wowed potential distributors (and me) with inexpensive Polaroid photos of people waiting 50 deep on lines to sample his product at seafood festivals. Inexpensive and very effective.

At all presentations, be prepared to volunteer information about

- What your product will do for the prospect's business
- Introductory offers
- Promotional features
- Ideas that will attract the prospect's salespeople and the salespeople of the prospect's clients

## Don't Jump at the First Opportunity

If your product is really good, distributors and stores will want you as much as you want them. Some distributors, like some stores, may not be right for your product. It doesn't help, for example, if distributors carry your product and make no real attempt to sell it. Resist temptation. Don't necessarily jump at the first offer. Make sure the distributor is right for you. When a large surgical supply distributing company offered to put our medical product in their catalog and sales sheets, we respectfully declined the offer. We thought its product line was too large and its salespeople would have no real incentive to sell our relatively low-margin product.

Careful probing of the distributor's situation is in order. Before marrying a distributor find the answers to these very important questions:

1. How will distributor salespeople greet the product and the price? It's a commonsense fact of life that salespeople will sell what's easiest and most profitable.
2. How will distributors advertise or communicate your advertising?
3. What will be the sell-through in the store? How will the distributors and the stores support your product?

This last point can be a real deal breaker and can cause particularly burdensome hassles. For example, Ragú Foods recently came out with a simmer sauce for chicken. Ragú had rolled out their advertising and spent big money on coupons. Yet, when I tried to find the product in my local grocery store, no clerk or cashier knew what the product was or even in what section it was placed. A consumer would have to be extremely persevering and really want the product to track it down.

Taking the time to find an ideal distributor is worth it. As your business grows, you'll find that the relationship you have with your distributor is one of the most important assets you can own.

**Slice of Life**

A distribution system may be so entrenched that you may be effectively embargoed from doing business in certain areas. The soft drink industry is like that in some regions of the country. Procter and Gamble purchased Hires root beer in an effort to develop a presence in the soft drink industry. Hires was a well-respected name with a long tradition of steady sales. Because they had a strong warehouse operation, Procter tried to bypass the independent bottling system. In an independent bottling system, the beverage company usually sells the syrup or the ingredients to the bottler while the bottler does the actual filling and merchandising. The soft drink industry is driven by these independent—very independent—bottlers. Not surprisingly, the bottlers weren't thrilled by Procter and Gamble's move to bypass them. Sales declined so drastically that giant Procter was forced to beg off and sell the brand.

In contrast, Barq's was a small, regional maker in the New Orleans area. After seven years of knocking on the doors of New York Metro bottlers, the company finally convinced a Seven-Up bottler to distribute its product. Barq's rapidly became the second-largest root beer in the country. By learning the salient points and subtleties of dealing with the existing beverage distribution system, little Barq's was able to outmaneuver the giant Procter and Gamble.

Selling just to move products is not an end in itself. You have to get paid for your product too. Sound obvious? It ain't.

Although you may be ecstatic getting your product into major, prestigious stores like Bloomingdale's or Macy's, the euphoria vanishes quickly when you realize you may have to wait 90 days to get paid or that Bloomingdale's may be wearing the latest in Chapter 11 outerwear. Neither alternative is great for cash flow. Your contact list will be of great value in finding out who pays in what length of time. (My experience with Dun & Bradstreet, usually the contact of first resort, has shown its ratings to be woefully inadequate.)

Once you've established yourself in the distribution chain, make certain the flow is smooth. If there are any problems, make changes immediately. Don't let a festering problem lie. Like a car with a faulty part, the problem won't heal itself. It will continually come back to haunt and harass you.

**Slice of Life**

Kreepy Krauly, a manufacturer of an automatic swimming pool cleaner, had a problem with declining sales. Competing companies were making inroads. They asked us to find out why.

We interviewed a number of swimming pool builders—the people who recommended and installed the Kreepy Krauly pool cleaners. They told us that they were no longer recommending Kreepy Krauly because sparse distributor representation and lack of service backup was causing erosion of the Kreepy Krauly image. There was also the matter of having to pay small, but frustrating, warranty charges. Although the Kreepy Krauly product was considered good, it wasn't worth the hassle of dealing with the company and distributors.

We recommended a constant flow of communications, trade show efforts, consumer brochures and an extended warranty. We told Kreepy Krauly management to actively and continuously demonstrate to builders that Kreepy Krauly wanted to help them sell pools.

Kreepy Krauly is now the leading automatic pool cleaner.

It sounds simple and obvious now, but without our interviews with the builders, the company would never have known the problem or the solution.

## Enthusiasm Is Contagious

Keep a constant flow of promotional creativity going to keep spirits and interest up. Low-cost ways to promote your product include consistent trade calls, in-store demonstrations, telemarketing, trade shows, flea markets, sampling, trial offers, free deals, premiums, and guarantees. Don't forget to target bottom-rung salespeople also. As we saw in the Ragú story, these people can help or hinder, depending on how much attention you lavish on them.

One final word about selling. Many entrepreneurs are afraid to sell to the mega-companies such as IBM, Xerox, or New Products Workshop (just kidding, readers). Frankly, they're intimidated. But the one thing most entrepreneurs forget is that companies don't buy goods and services. People do. You're not selling to a building or corporate entity but to a human being who works for a company and has basically the same goals, fears, and family responsibilities as you do. In fact, in developing new business for my company, I've found that presidents are the easiest sell. They have no one above them to impress!

*A sales training tip:* Here's an exercise I heartily recommend to remind you of the effectiveness of selling, and you'll also make enough money for a nice lunch. Next time you're at a resort and someone offers you a free gift (usually worth about $25) to listen to a time-sharing spiel, take the money. These people are good. Listen carefully to how the presentation is broken down—very similar to our presentation strategy.

The salesperson will spend the first part of the presentation asking questions and finding out your needs. Only at the very end of the presentation will you actually get to tour the property. The salesperson knows what's important to you because you gave the salesperson the answers. You told the salesperson your dream (and your objections) because you were asked.

Chances are, even if you had no interest in the offering going in, you'll have at least some when you leave. That's how effective good personal selling can be. But remember to leave your credit card at home.

## Selling to Supermarkets

Clever salesmanship and an innovative product can also save you big money when you try to get your product into large supermarket chains. Eventually, and particularly if you're in the grocery business, you're going to hear about a particularly nefarious creature called the "slotting allowance" monster. It's essentially a bribe you pay a supermarket chain to stock your new product. In my opinion, it's not only unethical, but it should be illegal. But it isn't and it won't be, because supermarket chains can "hide" the practice under a number of guises and euphemisms like "promotional allowances" and "stocking fees." One particularly greedy chain was even using their awesome leverage to "charge" people to make new product presentations to them.

Slotting allowances evolved when supermarkets decided they had a limited amount of shelf space, and why shouldn't they "maximize their resources," by essentially renting their sales space. The practice became a policy because manufacturers and distributors were all too willing to pay this legalized extortion. Major soft drink companies—you know who they are—are loaded with cash and are particularly favorable to this practice because it tends to exclude all but the major players.

One supermarket chain manager relates how he was offered big bucks from a major food manufacturer to move a certain product to a front aisle display in local stores for about a week—just long enough to impress the manufacturer's vice president, who was coming in for a visit.

Now that I got that off my chest, I should mention that slotting allowances are probably here to stay so we'll just have to deal with them.

*A moneysaving tip:* Slotting allowances can be worked around by a manufacturer without deep pockets. Here are some tactics that have worked in the past. I can't promise they'll work for you, but they're worth a shot.

- Sell your product so well or make your product so unique that a store would be crazy not to stock it.

- Plead poverty or ignorance. Don't laugh, my seafood client did this, and it worked.
- Give free products (two-for-one deals, etc.), additional quantities of goods, instead of money.
- Offer to do private label brands for the retailer. These are normally generic type products and can often help you secure more shelf space and provide a reference for consumers when comparing your brand to others.
- Plaster your market area with coupons to build store traffic.
- Create a consumer demand (like the Smartfood people in Chapter 4) that will force stores to stock your product.

Or forget the whole thing and investigate other means of distribution.

## Alternative Distribution Avenues

Entrepreneurs and new-product managers tend to get caught up in the details of running a business or are so close to the product that they get tunnel vision. For instance, if you're selling a food product and can't get stores interested, you can still sell to restaurants, schools and other institutions, vending machine companies, penal institutions, snack bars, mom-and-pop stores.

Or you build your own distribution chain. No fooling. Most people think of marketing only in the traditional wholesale-to-retail channels. But this is only an incredibly small part of the distribution channels available. Redken Products created a business built on loyalty by selling directly to beauty salons.

### Pop Quiz

You've invented a new windshield wiper and it's not selling well. Now what?

Look for the path of least resistance:

Lifetime Auto Products acquired the rights to market a unique three edge wiper blade—Tripledge Wipers. It was the first and only lifetime-guaranteed windshield wiper blade in the world. Although it had succeeded somewhat in test market, Jennifer Runyeon, president of Lifetime, thought the product had much more potential than it had demonstrated. Says Runyeon, "The old company had gone to the traditional automotive aftermarket trying to sell the wipers through retailers. Tripledge wipers, which cost $19.95 per pair, would be displayed next to the better known, less expensive blades (so) car owners (who) purchase new blades every six months would simply ask for the more inexpensive blades."

Tripledge could not compete. Runyeon then made a key distribution move. Instead of fighting harried dealers to sell the blade to consumers (and taking the path of most resistance) she marketed the product directly to consumers through catalogs, late-night commercials, credit card statement inserts, and print advertising. The company now ships 10,000 to 15,000 orders five days a week and employs 200 people.

Okay, you have fifteen thousand electric salad rinsers clogging your basement that nobody seems to want. What's a body to do? Sell direct.

## Direct Marketing

*Direct marketing* is an all-encompassing term meaning selling directly to the final purchasers. We can define it as a distribution system which elicits a direct response from the consumer, reducing the costly roles of stores and distributors. Direct marketing can include (but is not limited to) direct mail, continuity sales, telemarketing, home sales, direct selling, and multilevel marketing. In effect, the distribution system becomes an integral part of the product concept. You control the goods or service, packaging, advertising, promotion, merchandising, pricing, and storing. You actually establish, and in fact are, an independent channel of distribution. Direct marketing involves acquiring and motivating a body of consumers with whom you create a continuing relationship.

A program of direct marketing can lead to a whole new business system on which to build incremental future growth. It provides new opportunities to profit from the efficiency of marketing directly to highly targeted demographics—both with new products (possibly your salad rinser) and with existing products. Direct marketing provides the opportunity to sell higher-margin specialty items and to increase margins on existing lines. Plus, it provides the ability to do all this without the competition being able to read sales.

As a bonus, direct marketing is an efficient testing lab for new products to be marketed through the more traditional existing retail channels. You can quickly develop a benchmark on where sales should be and where they should be coming from. Once you have that important information, you can effectively target the right kind of store for your product. Since your product has developed a track record, you can exploit that fact in your sales presentations to stores and distributors. There is a vast subset of ways to market direct, limited only by your imagination. (See Table 7-1.)

**Table 7-1.** Direct (Alternative) Distribution Channels

| Channel | Advantages | Disadvantages |
|---|---|---|
| Through catalog merchants | Overhead limited to cost of goods | Often a seasonal business<br>Catalog merchant must sell your product at a high markup |
| Party plans | High markups the rule<br>Number of salespeople unlimited<br>Not capital-intensive | Highly saturated market in some areas<br>Amateur salespeople can be hard to manage, high attrition rates |
| Multilevel marketing | Very popular in recessionary periods<br>All distributors working toward common goal<br>Major incentives to build independent businesses<br>Not capital-intensive | Highly regulated<br>High attrition rates among salespeople<br>Constant effort to keep sales-people enthused<br>Similarity to illegal pyramid schemes |
| Program-length commercials | Fast results<br>Reach a great number of people at one time<br>Excellent for product demonstrations<br>High markup | Heavy up-front costs<br>Market becoming heavily saturated |
| Franchising your product | Captive, repeat buyers<br>Good geographic growth potential<br>Franchisees highly motivated | Tightly regulated<br>Heavy legal costs<br>Only some businesses lend themselves to this method |

**Through Catalog Merchants.** Direct mail companies are always looking for new ideas so that their catalogs will be considered newsworthy. You can sell your product outright to the catalog house and have them stock your product, or you can make arrangements to drop ship from your warehouse. In effect, the catalog company becomes your selling arm. One downside is that direct marketers require high markups, often four to six times cost. You'll have to try to keep your prices down to the bare minimum.

**Party Plans.** Tupperware and Mary Kay are now part of Americana. There's even a Tupperware Museum in Florida. The nation is always ready for new ideas that can be sold through parties. An untapped source that I've always believed in and that nobody is exploiting is men.

Why not sell hand and power tools at bowling parties, sports bars, card games, and other allegedly male-bonding activities?

**Multilevel Marketing.** This is one of the fastest growing segments of the direct marketing business. Even Fuller Brush, one of the last bastions of door-to-door selling, is going multilevel. It just announced the launching of a multilevel marketing program called "FullShare," to replace the firm's traditional marketing systems.

In a multilevel system, you essentially establish new people (call them Harry and Sally) in their own business, which is to sell your product. Harry and Sally are paid commissions. They in effect become independent distributors. Harry and Sally, in turn, recruit others (for instance, Ethel and Bob) to become distributors, and they recruit still others (Jeremy and Meredith et al.) to sell your product. For every sale made by this chain Harry and Sally get overrides. There are many variants on the multilevel system. This system obviously has great appeal in recessionary times as people want to control their own financial life in a business of their own.

The downside is that because of a great deal of fraud in the business and its similarity to illegal pyramid schemes, the business is (rightfully) fraught with regulations.

**The Infomercial.** The popularity of the program-length commercial is considered a relatively recent marketing phenomenon, yet it was widely accepted in the early days of television. Yes, people do buy hand-hammered Chinese woks at four in the morning. The program-length commercial has gained wide, if grudging, acceptance and generated a large volume of sales. Additionally, the immediate-response nature of the business (usually by phone) gives the marketer the rare ability to pinpoint sales and thus allows the flexibility to shift media dollars into high-performance markets rapidly. The downside is heavy upfront costs and market saturation as more and more companies enter the market.

**Franchise Your Product as a Service.** Let's say you have a new product that cleans driveways so they look new. You can, of course, sell your product to driveway cleaning companies or hardware stores. But why not create a franchised group of driveway cleaning companies featuring your patented and proprietary product? The downside is that not every product lends itself to this category, and franchising your business is tightly regulated. Legal costs can be high.

There's also another way to market your product which we're going to discuss at length in Chap. 11. Sell the whole nine yards to someone else and let them worry about it while you move on to something else.

## Summary

1. Creating a new product is simply one aspect of the new-product development picture. Selling and enthusiasm are just as important, if not more important, than the big idea.
2. It's just as important to get management of your company interested and sold on your undertaking as to get consumers excited.
3. Eliciting trade enthusiasm is important to keep your product selling throughout the sales chain.
4. It's feasible to create an entirely new distribution chain, if sales through existing channels are not working to your satisfaction.

## Questions, Answers, and Additional Insights

*But I'm not a high-pressure salesperson. In fact, I'm not a salesperson at all. To be honest, I hate selling. How can I get around this sales-driven atmosphere?*
High pressure is definitely not the way to go. A study by psychologists at the City University of New York gave fascinating proof why. People who switched insurance brokers were asked why they had done so. Only 16 percent blamed faulty or inefficient service. More than twice that percentage blamed the first salesperson for pressuring them. They resented it. When you question people and speak to their needs, you're not selling a product but helping prospects further their goals. When you do that, you are a welcomed partner, not an imposition.

*How do I find out who my distributors are and how my distribution systems work?*
Network in reverse. Find a similar product in a store and ask the clerk or manager who put the product in the store. Many store managers and clerks will be glad to help. Of course, trade magazines and trade associations are excellent sources of information. No matter how esoteric your product may be, there's bound to be a trade association, magazine, or special interest group that will be a great source of information.

*Our product is not achieving adequate shelf space. How do I react?*
Run, don't walk, out of your office and down to the distributor. Start creating new promotions and excitement. Small problems become large problems if you don't take immediate action. You should constantly be visiting new markets to see how your product is doing.

# 8
# Stalking the Perfect Name

*Chapter preview:*

- ***Attributes of a great name***
- ***Why puns should almost never be used (but often are)***
- ***The end-benefit promise of a great name***
- ***A dozen naming tips***

Gotcha. You're reading my words. Something about the name of this book must have captured your attention. Or perhaps it caught the attention of the person who gave the book to you. At any rate, somehow, in some way, the book's title—its name—started a chain of events that eventually brought you to this page.

A good name will catch you every time. *Branding* is the trade term for referring to the naming process. But whatever you choose to call it, the name of your product is what you are going to try to embed in the consumer's brain.

But it all started with the book's title—or name.

*Good names cajole, invite, and persuade your customer to pay for the product and take it home.* The helpful in-store salesperson has gone the way of the homemade apple pie and a vacant taxi on a rainy day (meaning you hardly see them any more). Your product's name and package have taken the salesperson's place.

*A good name functions as a headline on the shelf.* It reeks of consumer benefit. A product name shouldn't walk tenderly into the jungle fray. It should attack with the subtlety of a sharpened spear. The results of a great name are speedy trial and a positive feeling about your product.

*The good names are the simple ones that grab the consumer like the infamous hook at the old-time talent shows.* Naming your product leaves no room for subtlety. You simply can't afford it. Eventually you're going to stop dropping coupons and running commercials. Your product is going to have to sell itself.

Your objective is to grab the consumer so that the consumer reaches out and grabs the product, almost without realizing it. A good name prospects for the customer and invites the consumer to learn more. This is particularly important when your product is considered a staple or is in a category that has been driven solely by price (which, by the way, is often the sign of a lackadaisical marketer).

*A good name is memorable and distinctive.* Naming a product is a strategic decision. It reflects the company image. It is not a flight into fantasy. A name can be fun—in fact, very often it is fun—as long as it furthers a marketing goal.

A name can be downright serious and direct too. When an electronics customer is looking for an RX24 MicroChip with a xenerian crystal, simply calling the chip Fred is not going to close the deal. Or if your product is a high-price, serious-stakes car, you can be sure that the buyer is not going to want one called Buggsy.

*A good name differentiates your product from every other product.* It can also set your "parity" product apart from the also-rans. It can transform a loser into a winner.

Choosing the right name involves working with the consumer, as in everything we do. Product names are dynamic creatures. Some are fading from our lexicon as our language changes and as older products are supplanted by newer ones. Acceptable names even vary from one category to another depending on how the category is evolving. At one time if you asked for a seltzer, someone might bring you an effervescent analgesic like Bromo Seltzer. Now, the same request would result in a glass of bubbling water with a dash of fruit essence.

*A good name toys with our emotions.* Our emotions rule our life, and nowhere is this shown better than with the successful brand names of our times. Pampers (disposable diapers) is one of the great names for a product. It is loaded with consumer insight and feeling. Its very name says nurturing. The name positions the product to benefit the baby, and the mother's ego, by promising a drier baby. Sure, the surface reason for being of the product is convenience, but that's a given. The name Pampers instills added values and consumer motivations into the product and eliminates the guilt the mother might feel wrapping the baby in wads of paper and plastic.

A good name overcomes the barriers of product skepticism through raw emotion. You must do a lot of selling in the 16 or so seconds you own the consumer's attention on the shelf.

Unfortunately emotional benefit names don't always win the support of top management. Look at these abominations:

Lever 2000—soap. Cold and sterile. Who wants a soap for the year 2000 or one that sounds like it's loaded with chemicals when others infer security (Safeguard), sensuality (Caress), or softness (Dove) from the shelf?

New Breed—a dog food. How does it make the pet or its owner happier? To me it sounds like it came directly from R&D. The name might have appeal if the product was positioned for a new breed of dog.

Athena 2000—a sewing machine. Does the woman want a sewing machine full of bells and whistles for the year 2000, or does she want a machine that can aid her in creating new garments that she can be proud of? The name of a product addressed to women should "soften" high-tech features by making the features more accessible and less intimidating.

Jell-O 1-2-3—a dessert. This product has had two past deaths. Essentially the product creates an instant gelatin type dessert with three texture levels, hence the name 1-2-3. But why not create a name with appetite appeal? Just looking at the picture on the product gets across the fact that it has three layers. The name offers no added value, no appetite appeal.

Here's another of Feig's famous generalities. A product that's positioned to women should rarely be named by a number (there are some exceptions, like VO 5 by Alberto Culver and Chanel No. 5, but, by and large, these are products that have achieved share of heart in another time). Women seem to want more in the way of an emotional appeal. Men, however, are more responsive to naming a product by a number—especially a high-tech product like a car or a stereo. I'm sure there's a sexist explanation I can come up with, but I won't for fear of alienating half the readership (I won't say which half).

## A Good Name Builds Product Expectations

Past experiences with a brand, perceived quality, habits, even the time of day can affect a purchasing decision. "Get me a bottle of Anacin" might well be the kneejerk reaction of someone with a headache when the person really wants a bottle of aspirin. But the strength of the Anacin name built over many years of advertising drives the solution. As usual, we, as marketers must live and react to the way the market is and not the way we want it to be. The market, like the consumer, is ever changing.

A good name conjures up clear images in the mind of the consumer as to what the product is going to do. It will even add to the performance by creating a certain expectation. Food usually tastes better when it's enjoyed in a restaurant with a fancy name. Restaurateurs know that presentation of your dinner is a major contributor to the success of the meal.

The recipe for a great name is simplicity of imagery and an end benefit promise. This sounds an awful lot like share of heart and positioning, doesn't it? It should, because the product name is a major contributor to the Gestalt of your product, especially for an impulse-type product, like a candy bar, a pen, or certain cosmetics. In an impulse product the whole purchase decision is short-circuited. The consumer has no time to think, only react. Your name has to spur that reaction, which is how L'eggs pantyhose became the dominant force in the woman's hosiery market.

Thus, the ultimate goal of your naming (or branding) is to develop the brand name that makes the product or concept work best, that makes it interesting, appealing, and understandable to the largest segment of consumers. The brand name must provide strong motivation for the consumer to respond quickly and to purchase the product. Descriptors and even flavor names must act synergistically with the chosen brand name to advance the product concept.

The name should reflect the desired positioning of the product and communicate the benefits quickly and effectively, on the shelf, in advertising and coupons, and in all other merchandising and promotional material.

**Slice of Life**

A small northeastern dairy product company wanted to breathe some life into their American cheese product. It was primarily a heavily discounted product and driven by deals. Even though the product sold at a rock bottom price (actually a tad cheaper than a rock) neither consumer nor supermarket would buy. That is, until the company tried a new, simple marketing strategy. Instead of positioning their product with the traditional American cheese singles, we developed the concept of "Deli Singles." The package reflected this change. To further enhance the positioning of cheese freshly sliced at the deli counter (which is usually more expensive), the company actually charged 50 cents more per package. The result—new sales and a totally revitalized product.

In a way, a strong name conquers the information overload we talk about. It enables us to handle sensory overload, too, by substituting images for words. It gets across the product concept instantaneously.

Quite often a respected and established brand name is worth more than the factory that produces the product. It may even be worth more than the vaunted recipe or secret formula. You can invent a recipe in days, but it takes a long time to establish a brand name. Your competitors may be able to improve on your product, but they can't take your name. It's against the law. Baking soda is worth pennies on the open market but about a dollar in an Arm & Hammer box. Put the name Arm & Hammer on a detergent, room freshener, or toothpaste, and you're on the shelf being purchased by consumers to the tune of $340 million dollars or so per year. You can buy several quadrillion pounds of baking soda for that kind of money.

A name can actually drive a product. The perfume and wine spirits industries and even the movie industry are examples of businesses built solely on names. If Calvin Klein's hits of Eternity and Obsession were named something like RXP3 and RXP2 (like aromas are called in the fragrance factories), they probably wouldn't be nearly as effective. My local wine and spirits retailer suggests that a recognizable name and logo nets him at least three extra dollars per wine sale—even if it's a crummy wine. Seagram's 7 built its business on a simple phrase—"Seven and Seven" (the latter seven was for 7-Up). The impact of a name on the customer is enormous in the wine and spirits industry. When a person is in a bar, calling for a drink, the customer wants something easy to say and wants to feel special for ordering it.

Product names tend to go in cycles depending on the country's mood or the zeitgeist of the moment. In the creative revolution of the 1960s and 1970s there were Screaming Yellow Zonkers, Dippity Do, Herbal Essence, and a host of weird, fanciful names. But the (possibly) creative excesses of that time have reverted to the dull back-to-the-basics names of these more somber 1990s. In the 1970s and 1980s, we were big on florals and naturals. Today's names owe more to a copywriter's thesaurus and inane attribute studies than any real marketing skill or consumer insight.

### Pop Quiz

Of course, you instantly know what products are represented by Ivory, Tide, Arm & Hammer, Snuggle, and even I Can't Believe It's Not Butter. But, what products do these names represent?

1. Direct
2. Answer
3. Cue
4. Yes
5. Logics
6. Peak

*Answers:* (1) Household cleaner, (2) bank teller machine, (3) toothpaste, (4) laundry detergent, (5) line of hair care products, (6) yup, another toothpaste.

## Why a Good Name Is So Important

Names have to do more today because there are more products out there to sell. The consumer is not totally happy about this situation, because most of these products are "new, improved" and "do-alike" products which just make the job of shopping more complex. There is less chance to get your message heard over all the others.

How many brand names would you say try to get the attention of the average consumer each day? Ten? Twenty? Two hundred? Nope, not even close. The consumer is bombarded with over 10,000 brand names daily. Commercials, billboards, supermarkets—stores of all kind and products of all kind are constantly fighting for attention.

The advent of cable TV has also made it more important to make the name a potent selling force. Once upon a time, two years B.C. (before cable) advertisers could count on a flow of steady viewers and listeners. And most commercials were 60 seconds long. Advertisers such as Jell-O, Anacin, Texaco, and Alka-Seltzer could make a major impression by simply registering their images in the consumer's collective consciousness.

But with high advertising costs and an extremely segmented audience, the product name must identify with your target customer and work as hard at the point of sale as it does on a billboard. This is not as impossible as I'm probably making it sound, because most products are developed for a category that has its own set of buzzwords and expressions. Learning about these and keeping current is a necessary part of naming.

## Where Do the Best Names Come From?

Before our preoccupation with alleged linguistic databases, names of products came from everywhere. And everyone. The name for Ivory Soap came from the bible. Good old Harley Procter, founder of Procter and Gamble, was wracking his head trying to come up with a name for that soap that was so pumped full of air it floated. He wrote down hundreds of names until he went to church one day and heard the following words from a psalm spoken by his pastor: "All thy garments smell of myrrh, and aloes and cassis, out of ivory palaces whereby they have made thee glad."

And so (in the language of the bible) Ivory was begat. Now, I know that the bible was not written so marketers could sell soap, but if today's marketers had the chance, they would probably name the soap "Light n' Floaty." Can't you see the argument in the researchers room...."Let's see, ivory is hard. It comes from the mouth of an elephant which is an endangered species. No way."

Some names have been driven by the idiosyncracies of company heads. George Eastman of Kodak simply liked the sound of the letter k. Two Ks are better than one, he thought. Was Heinz 57 Varieties named because Heinz had 57 varieties? No. The founder just liked the numbers 50 and 7. (Heinz actually was selling more than 60 varieties when the name/slogan was introduced.)

Many of today's dull, lifeless names owe more to bytes than brains. Marketers are placing too much reliance on computers. In our office we have a fascinating computer program that will take almost every consumer attribute you desire and create names, phrases, and sounds based totally on these attributes. We furnished our offices with IBM compatibles just because the program sounded fascinating and we needed something to run it. The program works just like the ad said it would. It generates names. And generates more names. And more names. It will come up with names forever if you let it. There is just one eensy-weensy problem. We've never gotten a good name from it. The fact that we have the program goes over great in sales presentations to prospects, but it's never created a name that would achieve the client's goals. Unless, dear reader, you have a product that can be named Surblub, Srafdap, or Scrub My Urns.

The program lacks the human touch that's so necessary to name generation. The more your name can do from the shelf, the less you have to spend on continuous advertising.

Our best method for generating names is an old-fashioned one. Fear. It takes one strident, semihysterical call from me to the New Products Workshop (NPW) staff. "We have to have a name by 3:00 p.m. tomorrow afternoon or the client is going to cancel the project, and none of us will get paid." It works every time.

Earlier we talked about how our marketing team helped develop Glad Lock Bags. We also came up with the Glad Lock name. Sort of. Here's what happened. It was the midpoint of the project assignment (to develop and position this putative product). We knew we were on to something. Only we couldn't decide what to call the product. All the team members came up with names that they were immensely proud of. (None of these names were computer-generated either).

We had names like Snap Lock (the original name for the product in past incarnations), Color Change Bags, Green Seal Bags (with a picture of a green seal, the animal kind). We put these names on an easel, along with a description of the product benefits.

Consumers shot down all our names, quite enthusiastically. None of our names made the consumer want the product. So, in the grips of frustration, we asked the consumers what name would be best.

To them it was simple. They played with the product and looked at the benefits and names on the easel. "Well, it locks, right?" one woman, asked, running her finger up and down the seal. The moderator nodded. Another asked, "It's from Glad, which is a pretty good company, right?" The moderator nodded again. "Well, then why not call them Glad Lock Bags?"

So we're all sitting behind the focus room mirrors, all of us supposedly creative people, and we all look at each other. Why didn't we think of that?

We came up with the descriptor by ourselves. Sort of. One woman respondent after another would describe, somewhat sheepishly, how she would wash out self-locking bags and reuse them and that they would still close. So we called ours "recloseable bags." It was our way of identifying with the consumer. Glad Lock bags were the only product on the market making the (inferred) reusability claim.

## Don't Forget the Descriptor—It Should Sell Too

The name, coupled with a descriptor, must tell the complete product story. A *descriptor* is a key brand name component. It usually describes your product. It's the little blurb you put under your brand name to further describe the product and positioning. That may seem obvious, but too often the descriptor is treated like the president's brother. Nobody cares.

For instance, we were also evaluating Glad Lock sandwich bags. The problem was, if you don't got a sandwich, you probably don't need the bag. Putting the word "sandwich" near the name meant we were eliminating a major portion of the target audience who may or may not want a bag exclusively for sandwiches. It didn't make major sense to dilute the product premise.

Consumers buy what they see. If it connects with their life at that moment, they're interested. If it doesn't connect, they're not prospects for the product. They really don't want to think too much about their plastic bags when they have an hour of shopping left to do, a mortgage to pay, and kids to be chauffeured. Don't eliminate your market by overpositioning it or by narrowing it too much.

## The Psychological Benefits of an Established Brand Name

Of course, if you have a successful brand, that can be reason enough for a consumer to buy your product. If your first product or products were pleasing, then the consumer is probably going to want to sample your encore presentations.

Not to be underestimated is the concept of familiarity. When you attend a party with people you don't know, you gravitate to the person you know, the person you are familiar with. You might go home with someone different, but your first conversation or connection is with the person that's familiar to you, even if he or she is the second best of a mediocre lot. A brand name, like an acquaintance, eventually becomes a familiar, friendly face.

An existing brand name is loaded with the emotional baggage—both good and bad—of everything that's taken place before. In this case, determining the preconceived notion is vital, because it's the consumer's, not yours.

A marketing researcher told me about a set of automotive focus groups he ran with Volvo owners. One person after another had trouble of some kind with the car. But they didn't blame Volvo. They blamed themselves. Really. They each thought that they had gotten the only "bad" Volvo that has ever been sold. Almost all said that they would buy the car again—well, maybe not, after hearing what the other group members said. The point I'm making is that if the group had been Chevrolet owners, and one person in the group had a faulty speedometer, almost everyone would blame it on lackluster craftsmanship and "those idiots in Detroit." The Volvo owners blamed problems on themselves. That's how important a name and the quality imagery you instill it with is.

None of this is to exclude the witty name, the far out name. Screaming Yellow Zonkers and Orville Redenbacher's (yes, there really is an Orville Redenbacher) are still around after all these years.

The fun thing about names is that there are no right or wrong answers. That's why the key to finding the winning name is to constantly experiment just like we do with our entire new product development program.

Ask. Stimulate. Keep in mind that developing a name can get extremely personal. Naming is one of the few disciplines where even the most secure and decisive CEOs will ask for spousal approval. If the spouse thinks it sounds too much like a perfume or hair care product or a beloved deceased aunt, the CEO may shoot it down.

Here are the steps to creating the perfect name. Our methodology is a mix of creative name development and a great deal of consumer feedback to make sure that the name is truly consumer driven.

1. Examine the brand's prospective market from the perspectives of competitive framework and category names, relevant market trends, existing and potential consumer usage, strategic imagery possibilities. You can get most of these data by visiting stores, looking through catalogs, leafing through trade magazines, and visiting trade shows.

2. Get possible names from everyone. Your advertising agency, your suppliers, the receptionist, everyone. You can even get an idea or two from a linguistic database program!

3. Create prototype packages of your product with the various names. Don't scrimp on the artwork because we want to make things as easy and realistic for the consumer as possible. Also create rough ads and miniature billboards with the product (and the name). You want to make sure that the name will stand out in the 6 seconds that the average billboard is noticed.

Now, create overlays with the different names of your product. Using the same methods described in our research section, show the stimuli to consumers using the overlays to show different names in the same ads. (See Fig. 8-1.)

Put your names on competing products. Use competing names on your products. This will ensure that your names are adding value, beating the competition and furthering your goals. Always put a TM (trademark) on your new names before they are shown to consumers to aid you if there are any legal challenges down the road.

Create a realistic shelf display with your product name and your competing product's name. Make sure (by watching consumers react) that your package stands out on the shelf and is the first one chosen.

4. Assess relative consumer interest in the names and concepts in terms of purchase interest, imagery, reinforcement of product positioning, flexibility, and fulfillment of product objectives. Use consumer groups and one-on-one interviews as before.

5. Modify, delete, and add names based on the results of consumer probing. Evolve, define, and recommend the optimum names and positionings for generating consumer interest and trial.

When the consumer gets excited, you have a winner.

**Figure 8-1.** Using concept boards to experiment with names and visual cues (pages 163 to 175).

**Figure 8-1.** (*Continued*)

**Figure 8-1.** (*Continued*)

**Figure 8-1.** (*Continued*)

**Figure 8-1.** (*Continued*)

**Figure 8-1.** (*Continued*)

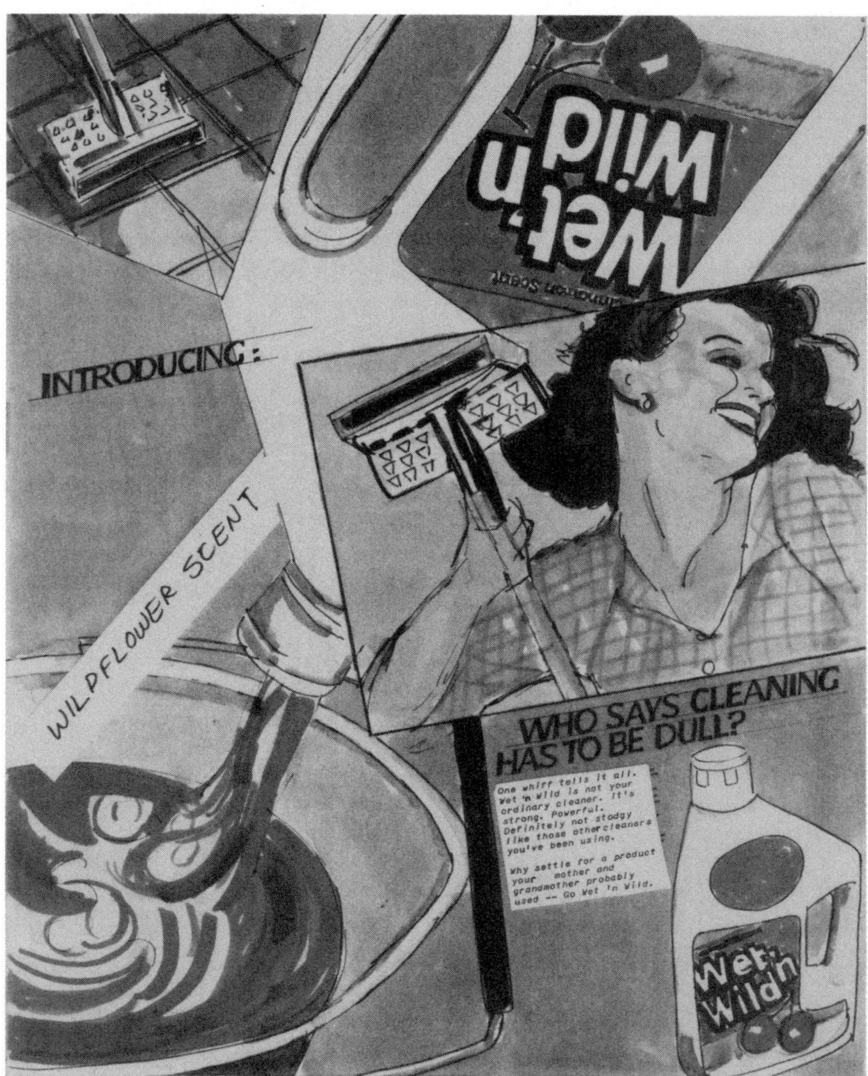


**Figure 8-1.** (*Continued*)

**Figure 8-1.** (*Continued*)

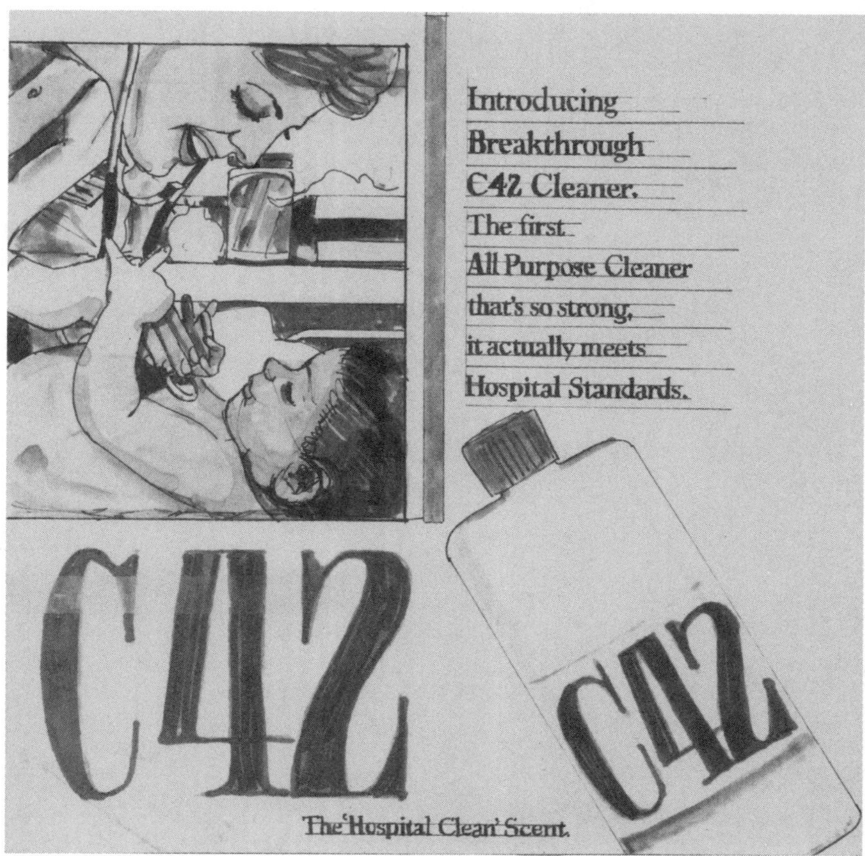


**Figure 8-1.** (*Continued*)

**Figure 8-1.** (*Continued*)

**Figure 8-1.** (*Continued*)

**Figure 8-1.** (*Continued*)

**Figure 8-1.** (*Continued*)

## Developing Line and Brand Extensions

Leveraging an existing brand name is a quick and useful way of creating awareness for your product. The myth has already been created. The value is already perceived by the consumer.

The best way to gauge the elasticity of a brand name is to physically attach the name and logo to a range of products and advertising materials and present these to consumers. Don't be afraid of stretching things too far, because the consumers will rapidly tell you what works and what doesn't. Building your product from an existing brand is like the old joke about how to sculpt an elephant: You take the block of marble and simply chip away everything that doesn't look like an elephant.

Your criteria in determining which brand name to use and which extensions are feasible is surprisingly simple. Would the extension make the consumer more likely to try the product? Does it reflect positively on your brand as a whole?

## Questions to Ask Before You Commit

Choosing a name for your product is a piece of cake. Choosing the right name is a great deal more problematical. Here is a checklist and some guidelines for naming your product.

- Will the name contribute something special to the success of the product?
- Will the name elicit trial?
- Does the name ask for the order? A name shouldn't just sit on the shelf pining for a buyer, it should actually call any prospect who is looking in the category. Adding the name "Sesame Street" or "Disney," for example, to a kid's toy gives it major impetus for a grandma purchase. That's why Disney is picky about licensing. It's an overwhelming equity. A tremendous moneymaker.
- Does the name add value to the product? The name should be a value-added proposition. It should add to the glamor of your product or else you might as well be selling generics. But even the generic advertisers are using creative names. D'Agostino's, an upscale supermarket chain, has introduced its own branded product under the name President's Choice.
- Does the name describe the product's benefits in a convincing way? You get to audition once. The name must act like a résumé getting the consumer to delve into the product further. Aunt Jemima's Pancake

Express (add water to the container and pour for instant pancakes) is a great example of this.

- Does the name reflect and enhance the product's performance cues quickly, vividly, and effectively? A good name gives the consumer something to look for and sets the stage for consumer usage. It tells consumers what to expect, why they should expect it, and why the product is better than the competing products. Sony's Walkman, although a bit awkward on the tongue, accomplishes the goal to perfection.
- Is the name flexible enough to allow for line extensions and original enough to be remembered? This whole book has been written under the assumption that your company is going to be around for awhile. A strong name is an equity you can build a business on. Hershey's has just launched Reese's Peanut Butter and is getting good trial from Reese's Peanut Butter Cup fans.

The best names promise security and empathize with the target consumer's life experience. The newly mass-merchandised adult incontinence category owes a lot to names like Depend and Serenity. They promise security without talking down to the consumer. The consumer must be able to react with the product mentally while in the aisle.

Here are a dozen additional guidelines and thought starters:

1. Start your trademark checks and searches as soon as possible and register anything that sounds even remotely close to the desired names.
2. Try to avoid puns. You may think you're clever, but few people will understand them. A friend of mine owns a local optical shop called O.I.C. Optical. After a decade, only myself and his immediate family understand that O.I.C. is supposed to mean "Oh I See."
3. Create a myth around your product name. Chicken was just a commodity item until Frank Perdue made his name and face a legend. (It's really beyond the scope of this book, but I think Frank is looking more like his products every year.)
4. Giving your product a name that denotes more than is in the box is a great way to ingratiate yourself to the consumer. Dove soap, Opium perfume, and Eternity all promise fantasy and magnify the buying experience. What woman wouldn't be entranced by a product called Moon Drops?
5. But don't overpromise and underperform. Fantasy is an illusion, but a margarine called "I Can't Believe It's Not Butter " had better taste like butter.

6. Don't be afraid to use long names. Art directors loathe them and marketing books usually recommend against them, but so what? If it breaks out of the ordinary and it turns on the consumer, don't worry about it. Orville Redenbacher doesn't exactly roll off your tongue, and many consumers don't believe he really exists, but his name helped develop the myth that became a magnet for popcorn lovers.
7. Try to avoid names with an "'n," and/or ampersands. They're usually trite 'n' dull. They're usually a coward's way out and a cop-out unless you can combine words in a particularly sexy way. What are Nice n' Easy and Clean & Smooth?
8. If you are going to use a proprietary company name (like Golds, Hampton, etc.) make your product stand out with an exciting descriptor. If you're in business long enough, the descriptor will carry over into everything you do and become part of your unique image.
9. Don't confuse simplicity with lack of motivation. Snuggles (fabric softener) is one of the truly great names of the 1980s.
10. Offbeat names can be effective when they balance an in-crowd ambience with your present and future marketing goals.
11. Coined and made-up words (like Corolla, or even Citizen, in the context of electronics) can work because they give you a blank slate to create your own emotion around. We created a name called Vivante for Coca Cola's now defunct Wine Spectrum unit. Consumers were unanimous—great name, wretched wine.
12. Give your product a new name that consumers either love or hate. Stay away from neutral names with no emotional value. Bully Toilet Bowl Cleaner arouses major negatives, but to consumers it really sounds like it will work.

Don't compromise on your product's name. Make sure it's great.

## Summary

1. Few new products today are "eagerly awaited," but we can pretend they are and make the consumer think so too, with a strong name. The name of your product is the first thing the consumer is going to see. The name is going to be associated with the product throughout the product's life. It's no time to settle for a compromise choice.
2. Good, effective names can come from everyone as long as you keep an open mind.

3. A good name creates expectations and satisfies the need of the consumer even before the consumer takes the product home.
4. A strong name sets the stage for line extensions and additional new products.
5. Although there is often a temptation to use puns and clever word plays, they can often backfire by going over the purchaser's head.

## Questions, Answers, and Additional Insights

*What are some of the disadvantages of using your name for line extensions?*
A poor performance on a branded product may sully your core brand's reputation. Even a well-thought-out line extension can cannibalize the brand. That's what happened when Miller introduced Miller Lite. Now both Miller Lite and the core brand—Miller High Life—are declining.

*What's the matter with choosing a name just because I like it? After all, that's the way it has always been done.*
There's nothing basically wrong with it, but we have found that consumers are better equipped to make the decision because they will be buying the product.

*If a name has to be simple, how do we account for names like Häagen Daz and Orville Redenbacher?*
The imagery must be simple and quick. The name can be as long as you like or as hard to say as you would like as long as it contributes to the image you are trying to get across. One exception, however, is in a brand you have to ask for by name to purchase; for instance, in a tavern, consumers want something quick, easy, and sophisticated.

# 9

# Power Pricing Strategies

*Chapter preview:*

- ***Why "MBA pricing" is wrong***
- ***Pricing for consumer-perceived value***
- ***Why pricing too low is as fatal to sales as pricing too high***
- ***How to build prestige through pricing***
- ***The supermarket (or department store) as research lab***
- ***How to learn how to price your product by talking to the consumer***
- ***Making sure everybody gets a good deal***

By this time, I'm sure you've done your MBA-type homework. You've computed your spreadsheets and your P&L's (profit-and-loss forecasts). You've factored in all your costs and have worked up your five-year business analysis and marketing strategy. You've taken into account your costs of materials investment and your warehousing capabilities as well as your prospective labor costs. Now, incorporating the standard industry markup, you have prepared a worksheet of pricing differentials so you know what to charge your customers in order to get a fair return on investment for your company.

Put all these sheets of paper in front of you. Now crumple each of them into a ball and throw them at the nearest bean counter. We don't do MBA math here. Here we price by perceived value. Not yours, of course, but the consumer's. I'm not going to suggest you sell each widget for less than it costs to make and make up for it on volume. But I am going to suggest that you develop pricing strategies based on consumer needs. And that you spend more time talking to the people you expect to buy your product and less time to managers and controllers. Actually, since you just pelted the controller with a barrage of paper missiles, he's probably not talking to you anyway. All for the good.

Of all the parts of the new-product development process, pricing is probably the most elastic, the one that's easiest to control. As we've mentioned, consumers don't care if you make a profit or if you ever make another product as long as they get something at a price that they're willing to pay. To do this you have to treat the marketplace as a living, breathing world made up of varying segments that are constantly evolving.

The consumer marketplace is made up of four different categories:

1. *Things we don't want.* No pricing strategy is going to help these.

2. *Staples—essentials we need for basic survival.* These include products such as milk, bread, electricity, gas, and basic school supplies. Even low-priced cars. This category could also include pet food and computer disks (once we have the computer). In their basic form staples are usually price shopped unless the marketer instills the products with additional value. The trick is to move these products into the next sphere where consumers will actively seek out your brand.

3. *Things it might be nice to have.* These are nonessentials that are highly desirable but are not usually essential. They are actively sought out by the consumer or business. They include items such as prepared food, restaurant meals, mid-priced cars, conveniences for babies. This category might even include an investment purchase, e.g., new machinery for an industrial company. This is where the bulk of spending is and where most of the new products are developed. Competitive pricing is the rule. Goods have to be priced relative to competing products, and products must be priced to fit within a consumer's budget and mindset.

4. *Things we want desperately.* Most of the products in this category require an emotional commitment from the consumer which exceeds the physical worth of the product. Decisions to purchase products in this category are either, ironically, well-considered purchases or impulse items. The high-ticket items usually must be justified with a heavy dose of rationalization by the buyer. For instance, a Mercedes automobile is almost always rationalized as being bought because it has great engineering. Mercedes goes to great lengths to justify this thinking. This category also includes what we call little luxuries such as rich desserts or special cosmetics.

Take these scenarios, or paradoxes:

At one time it would have been considered obscene to pay $1.50 for one cookie or brownie.

Who would be silly enough to spend $7.50 for a shampoo when you can get a product that performs just as well for 99¢?

What sort of horrible person would spend $150 on an electronic kid's toy when consumers are complaining that they can't afford to gas up the family car?

> What kind of crazed spendthrifts would spend $40 on a pound of salmon from a catalog (plus shipping) when they can get fresher seafood from their local fish market for a fraction of the cost?
>
> Why would people spend $70,000 on a Mercedes when they could get a perfectly serviceable car for about 10 percent of the price?

Only weirdos. Like you and I and the mainstream of the U.S. population. Each of these instances represents a value to a certain, very targetable segment of consumers. Pricing for value is as much about learning human nature as it is about determining raw materials cost.

Hold it, you're probably thinking (or else you're trying to dig up a new brownie recipe). How can any of these represent value? They're all overpriced goods with giant-sized margins or they can be bought cheaper elsewhere.

The problem is that most marketers have no idea of the meaning of the word *value.* None. I bite my tongue when I hear a marketer talk about something called value. It's an absolutely superfluous term when used by a marketer.

Since I've been out of college, I've heard companies talk about value like it's a new concept. They don't get it. In almost every large company I've worked with, at least one person will stand up and speak words that I'm sure he thinks are quite visionary. "Let's preempt that segment of the market that wants 'quality and value.'" As if any segment has an overwhelming urge for the wretched and second rate.

*A low price, or "value" positioning, is no excuse to rob the consumer.* Unfortunately, in many so-called value products, the active ingredient or performance qualities have been reduced along with the price. You can't scrimp on quality to save a customer money, especially in the branded packaged good business. Quality is a given, a lower price should be treated as a bonus.

## Value-Added Pricing

*Value* is a marketing word. It's not a consumer word. Value isn't something you put in a product, like an extra mushroom or chocolate chip. It's what the consumer gets out of the product. I can't even remember hearing the word *value* used by a consumer unless some poor misguided researcher asks a question like, "Do you want value in a product?" It's hard to answer that question no. "No, all things being equal, I'd rather be ripped off." Long after the price is forgotten, the consumer's memories of your brand's effectiveness (or ineffectiveness) will remain. *Value is the perceived reinforcing cues the consumer receives from making and using the product.*

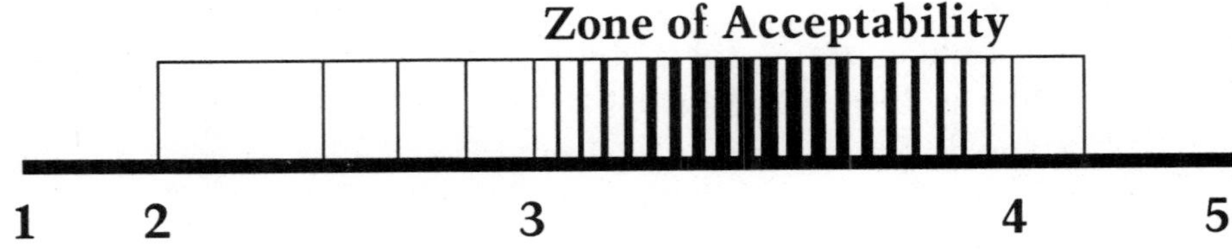


**Figure 9-1.** Similar to the positioning continuum, the pricing continuum defines the boundaries of your product. 1=too downscale—low perceived value; 2=price-intensive, bare-bones product—high-volume sales needed; 3=medium pricing—heavily competitive; 4=high pricing—low volume; 5=too upscale—outside consumer's financial limits.

Consumers usually make mental equations about what they're willing to pay for a product. I don't mean they do any mathematical wizardry, but when they shop they have a rough range of prices in their heads. The range varies based on past experiences, lifestyle, and how the consumers feel at a given moment. The range varies from category to category and even from store to store. Let's go back to the positioning continuum (Fig. 9-1). Only now we're going to call it a pricing continuum. Depending on the consumer's unique persona, an acceptable price can fall anywhere in the continuum.

A product is usually priced in one of three ways relative to a category:

1. High-price range
2. Mid-price range
3. Low-price range

All three price ranges have their strong points and their drawbacks for the marketer. The bulk of new products fall somewhere in the mid-range pricing. The niche opportunities lie at either pole. The right pole is high profit, high markup, low volume; the left is low markup, profit by volume.

To the right of the continuum are what might be called little luxuries. Little luxuries are discretionary purchases. They're part of almost every category. They fall in the "things we want desperately" category—if only for the moment. They're often impulse purchases because the consumer gets caught up in the emotion of the moment without benefit of a logical thought progression. In almost every category, an inspired marketer has taken a basic product, attached a higher price, and created a special niche. Look at Grey Poupon, Absolut Vodka, and the new craze in expensive fountain pens.

Consumers tend to look up to higher-priced products for transferred prestige. They remember these products better than the mass of products in the middle ground. David Weiss, president of Packaged Facts, a New York–based research firm, puts it this way: "The best way to market a product is not always with a mass market mentality."

But many marketers continue to price their products for the middle ground, even though it's a far more difficult route to take, especially for the manufacturer without megabucks. A far more logical positioning is to take the high road. If your product is better than the competition (or even if it's merely different) charge more for it. Make sure there's enough of a price differentiation between your product and others like it so that consumers realize they're paying for a better product. Use pricing as a merchandising tool to drive a superiority wedge between you and the competition. Retailers will love you for it; consumers might think you're something special. This pricing strategy works if your product offers a unique reinforcement cue (packaging, richness, a new taste, prestigious consumer equity) that is readily discernible—like the glitzy packaging of Godiva chocolates.

Pricing for the low road can also be an effective strategy, but it is fraught with more risks than you might expect. It is actually the pricing strategy that offers the least flexibility. There is always the danger of being hit with higher raw materials cost and losing the price advantage. You also risk being undersold by your competitor and being price-shocked until you drop by larger, better-financed competitors who can withstand the lower prices. That's one of the reasons People's Express airlines collapsed. When People's tried to expand into new routes, the larger airlines, particularly American, started noticing and matched them in price. Peoples, a no-frills airline, simply could not compete on service nor did they have any other kind of consumer equity to fall back on. American was able to absorb the losses to get rid of the pesky competitor. Large companies tend to ignore the low end competitor as an elephant ignores a flea. But once that flea draws blood—squoooosh. Low-priced products are also prone to being second guessed by consumers. "How good could it be if it's that cheap" is the usual refrain.

It's much easier to go down in price than to go up. Consumers will also readily accept a price drop rather than a price rise, especially if you're starting from a higher base. Plus, the higher prices give you more room to maneuver with deals and promotions to keep the product alive and vibrant. Even had it survived American Airline's swipes, chances are People's Express would never have found consumer acceptance at realistic pricing levels.

Right now, especially in the supermarket warehouse clubs and in the drug and beauty superstores, there is something called EDLP (every day low pricing). In theory, the stores buy at the rock bottom lowest price and sell at the rock bottom lowest price. But even they depart from the strategy and have promotions to generate interest. If you are priced too low, you don't have the flexibility to deal.

## Pricing for Staple or Survival Products

Let's look at some of the other factors that go into pricing by value. Essentially, the more a product is purchased, especially in the "need to survive" grouping, the more you can expect consumers to look for the lowest prices. Examples are milk, sugar, gasoline. None of these is a subject of great consumer interest. Because of the tremendous competition, the marketer is usually forced to come up with promotions or to drop prices further to move products.

But not always. Even a staple can be moved from the survival sphere to the "nice to have" sphere. If the consumer has just bought a flashy car, then he or she is probably quite willing to trade up to a high-octane blend of gasoline for this "baby" or purchase expensive extras like a CD player or special floor mats.

In the survival category, manufacturers have to work hard and continuously to convince the consumer to spend more on their product so it won't be as price intensive. That's what we mean by the value-added approach. Procter and Gamble tried to add value when they added calcium to their ailing Citrus Hill Orange juice to support a higher price.

## Desire for Status

Consumers often buy a product for symbolic reasons. They often equate price with self-esteem. That's why premium brands of liquor continue to sell well, even in a recession and even in low-income areas. This is not just a Western characteristic either. China, before it was semimodernized, had the most egalitarian society in the world. The primary transportation mode was bicycles. Yet there was a black market for counterfeit labels of the most prestigious bike models in much the way people here show off fake Rolex watches and Gucci bags.

The desire for status shows particularly in the pricing for credit cards. We ran focus groups for American Express with green card holders, gold card holders, and platinum card holders. There was a major caste system going on in the room with people sitting together based on the color of the cards and the yearly fees attached to them.

### Where Is the Consumer's Money Coming From?

A subtle factor that can affect your pricing strategy is determining which pocket the money is coming from. Ernest Potischman, a respected new-product consultant, tells about an assignment he handled for Gillette. Gillette had wanted to assess the effect different packaging motifs would have on a woman's intent to purchase a foot deodorant. Women were given a choice of two packages—one with an obviously feminine foot and one with a more neutral graphic. The women opted for the neutral approach, even though they admitted they would be the ones who would be using the product. The reason was that the product was going to be purchased in the supermarket with money taken from the family household budget. They considered it a selfish purchase, and they wouldn't spend the extra money. The neutral graphic made the purchase seem less selfish.

## Pricing for Convenience

This is probably going to surprise you, but consumers are loathe to pay extra for convenience. The microwave oven industry didn't really get started until bright-eyed marketers talked to the consumer. Women, one after another, told marketers that they were nervous about the new technology. And besides, who needed something that cooked faster? They wouldn't pay for this convenience. They neither needed nor wanted the product. Sales started cooking (I couldn't resist the pun) when marketers created interest in the technology on the part of men. Men like the idea of a supergizmo in the kitchen. So marketers learned to sell the "mirrors and blue smoke" of the jet age appliance to men and the benefits of quick defrosting to women.

## Pricing for Esthetics

What is a work of art worth? Whatever someone will pay. Consumers will pay a premium for esthetics or a convenience *they can rationalize in some secondary way*. The value is the good inner feeling they get from using the product. You can't put a dollar value on artwork or esthetics. It's a part of the complete buying experience.

*Price barriers are always changing as categories and markets evolve and consumers soften up.* At one time, it would have been obscene to pay $140 for what is essentially a kid's game. But Atari created a new ball game in the mid-1980s with the Atari 2600 when they broke a psychological price barrier. They did this by getting the parents interested in the games. The newly developed video games were not seen as kids' toys but rationalized as family products. Dad got the same kick out of Atari that his father used to get playing with your electric trains. Atari established a new pricing benchmark. After Atari broke the pricing barrier, many games and toys came along and were priced relative to Atari. Parents were no longer totally reluctant to spend the money. Nintendo now sells to kids and no longer worries about the almighty gatekeeper.

Product-line pricing is a function of intuitive judgment as well as consumer needs. Constant monitoring of your industry is essential. It's important to follow the trends and traditions of your product category. In the electronics industry, ultra miniaturization means higher prices. In the fragrance and wine and spirits industry, high price correlates with prestige and social safety. Even among the poor and even in a recession, premium brands continue to sell well.

A time-tested method for established companies is to have products at each of the major price points—high, medium, low—with features or product size being the key variable.

You might find it's even better to almost give the product away and sell the accessories. Manufacturers have learned that they can make more money on soap and paper towel refills than on dispensers, so they actually give the dispensers away. King Gillette learned long ago that they could sell a lot more razor blades than razors.

Choosing the right price means:

- Retailers and distributors will handle your product and give it the attention it deserves.
- You can make money to further your ventures.
- The consumer perceives that the price is reasonable for the value received and will patronize your product.

Here are some guidelines to help you with the pricing strategy.

### A Genuinely New Product Commands the Highest Prices of All

- There's no competition.
- Consumers have no frame of reference to establish a value in their own mind.
- Consumers who consider themselves "innovators" want to be the first on the block and on the cutting edge and will pay top dollar.

This is an artificial marketing situation, however. Sooner or later (actually much sooner than later), the bubble will burst. Other marketers will see the potential, enter the market, and prices will drop. That's why we say you should be working on improvements and new products even before the first one has been produced.

*Other Times to Price High*

- When you have a brand that's been traditionally priced for an upscale market and the product offers strong value-reinforcing cues.
- When you want to establish snob appeal.
- When your product is demonstrably better than the competition and incorporates features you're sure the consumer wants and is willing and able to pay for.
- When you have a product that offers security in a social setting.
- When you have an upscale brand that is traditionally higher priced than competitive brands.
- When you have a strong safety or security story to tell that would make people feel neglectful for choosing a "cheaper" (read "inferior") product.
- When you move a product from a typically low-priced category and reposition it for a new use in a typically higher priced category. Take the case of hydrogen peroxide. When sold in big brown bottles as a commodity, it can cost under $1.00. Refine it further for disinfecting contact lenses, and you can charge almost four times as much for a third of the quantity.

*Advantages of the High Price*

- Larger return on investment
- Building of upscale equity
- Excellent flexibility

*Disadvantages of the High Price*

- May be too high for market
- Usually more advertising and/or packaging expenses
- Relatively low volume of sales
- May be sensitive to difficult financial times

### When to Price for the Middle Ground

- When you're knocking off a higher-priced product.
- When you don't have a major new benefit to offer.

- When your product is not an impulse item and a consumer has many choices.
- When a product is "new to your business" but is firmly established in the consumer's mind.
- When you have a mid-priced equity that cannot be extended into a high-end product. It would be hard (if not impossible) to change a mid-priced Chevy Celebrity into a high-end automobile.
- When you have a repackaged product that has not broken any new positioning ground.

*Advantages of Mid-range Pricing*

- Consumers have adapted to this price—less price resistance.
- This is where the bulk of new-product successes are.
- Advertising and products can talk about benefits instead of price.

*Disadvantages of Mid-range Pricing*

- Highly competitive.
- Consumers have wide range of choice.
- Competitors likely to try and knock your product off by discounting or improving on your product.

### When to Price Low

- When you can produce a product at less cost than anyone else
- When your consumer equity is in a low-priced positioning
- When you're selling with a generic name instead of a brand name
- When you can obtain a major advantage by selling a no-frills product or want to fill out a product line (high, low, medium price points) such as a bare bones Walkman to compete with other personal stereos that might have more features but an inferior brand name

*Advantages of Pricing Low*

- Area of least resistance for selling to consumers and retailers. Everyone likes a bargain.
- Good for plain vanilla versions of products, particularly for imports from countries with low labor costs.
- Fewer advertising costs—price driven.

- Usually good trial.
- Builds volume quickly.

*Disadvantages of Pricing Low*

- Retailers may add extra markup, robbing you of positioning strength.
- Difficult to build quality equity with consumers.
- Consumers will often doubt the effectiveness or quality of your product.
- Competitively difficult, other companies will eventually undercut you.
- Product may actually sell out too quickly, leaving the distribution chain with a major gap that someone else may fill.

Pricing doesn't happen in a void. It is based on competitive pressures, consumer reactions at the moment of purchase, and the general state of the economy. That's why you must keep a constant eye on the marketplace and the consumer.

Here's how to determine the right price for your product:

1. Take a field trip. Visit supermarkets, department stores, malls, and specialty shops in as many geographic areas as feasible. Get a range of prices for products in your category. How do your product's features stack up?

2. Visit distributors, merchants, and salespeople. Find out the customary discounts and commissions. Be careful about taking their pricing advice, however. They will invariably suggest a low-price strategy because it's easier for them to sell and they can buy the product from you cheaper.

3. Develop concepts like we did in our research methods (in fact, all of this can be done at the same time you do your consumer research). Prepare a range of price stickers. Show prices that are even higher than you expect to charge to make sure consumers really think it a value. Do the same with the boards you have created for competing products.

4. Assemble groups of varying demographic segments (your interviewing facility will do this for you). Probe consumers on intent to purchase at each of the prices; how often they would buy the product; what product it would replace; and from what funds the purchase would come from—household budget, mad money, savings account, splurge money, and so on. Never ask a consumer what he or she would pay for your product without a direct reactive device like a price sticker. This ain't "The Price Is Right." Usually the consumer will say something ridiculously low and invalidate your price questions.

5. Now show the respondent the actual product, if available. Do the taste and reinforcing cues measure up?

Price is as much a part of the whole new-product picture as the name and the packaging. Although there are a great many theoretical pricing formulas, the best rule to follow is to price your product so that you can make money, your distributors can make money, and consumers feel like they are getting a good deal.

## Summary

1. Pricing a product is more a function of intuitive judgment and applied psychology than it is a function of cost of materials. As a product becomes familiar to the consumer, prices may drop but segmentation opportunities will often present themselves.
2. Each profit category has its own pricing requisites and profit margins that are as much a function of tradition as of any hard and fast rule.
3. Pricing is an elastic merchandising tool that should be used to help sell product and competitively position the product in the marketplace.

## Questions, Answers, and Additional Insights

*If a low price is so unimportant, how do you account for the effectiveness of couponing?*
A low price is important, but it is only one of the elements that go into making the purchase decision. A coupon-and-rebates offer provides a short-term trial to build awareness—after that the product is on its own; the lowest price won't sell a product that doesn't work.

*But I have always learned that pricing should be in direct correlation to what it costs you to make the product. Shouldn't manufacturing costs determine the product's eventual price?*
Consumers aren't interested in your costs. They are interested in what it is going to cost them. Here are two stories.

1. Remember, Henry Ford didn't sell cars at about $500 because he was able to make them that cheap. He knew he could sell a car at

$500 *if* he could make them that cheap. The consumer's wants and needs drove the product, not the other way around.

2. When Akio Morita, president of Sony, set about developing the Walkman, he was told by his engineers the product would cost the consumer over $200. He told his staff to get the price down to about $100 because that's what the consumer (his target audience was young adults 18 to 30) could afford and would pay without a great deal of price resistance.

# 10
# Turning Dross into Gold

*Chapter preview:*

- ***No product is perfect—how to turn dross into gold***
- ***Looking at negatives in new, positive ways***
- ***Looking at product negatives through the consumer's eyes***
- ***Turning by-products and waste products into profit centers***
- ***Changing consumer perceptions and building consumer fantasies***

Let's face it. Marketing is not always easy. Disasters can occur. Misjudgments can be made. Opportunities can be neglected. But it's in these circumstances that the real marketers shine. This chapter is about getting in touch with yourself and your business and dealing with real-world problems and solutions in nonobvious ways. It's also about discovering your equities and leveraging them to their fullest.

Take a good, long look at yourself, your product, and your business. What are you actually selling? What is your product? No, really. This is not a trick question. Arm & Hammer used to think they were selling baking soda. They found out they aren't. Arm & Hammer is really selling, and consumers are buying, the security and the implied power of the Arm & Hammer name and the yellow Arm & Hammer box. When they discovered this, management created a $340 million dollar household product business that had virtually nothing to do with baking soda.

The makers of Stolachnaya and Absolut Vodka aren't selling a clear, tasteless, potent liquid. Consumers are buying an image of savoir faire and prestige.

Disney is not selling rides or even a vacation, but an image of escape, dreams, memories, and good times. When you get the family photos back from Cinderella's Castle you probably forgot the one-hour waits for the rides, the soda that was splashed on your new Mickey Mouse sweatshirt, and the kids' crying for another ice cream cone. At least until the Visa bill comes in, you probably even forgot the thousand-dollar price tag.

You can create a success from even the dullest product in the dullest category if you stay in touch with yourself—and the consumer. One marketing person's dross can be another one's gold. (Dross is what you get when all the good stuff is gone—the perceived leftovers of the marketing world.) Dross may be products from another time. They may be products that some call "parity." They may be products in categories that some call "low interest." They may be products that suffered a "consumer disaster," like the lacing of Tylenol capsules with poison. They even may be by-products (that some call "garbage") of a manufacturing process. The gunk (that's the technical term) left over from the oil drilling process eventually evolved into Vaseline. The name Vaseline eventually became one of the most respected assets in the world.

The key is to learn what you have, and what you don't, and to build creatively from this knowledge base. Trouble is, a lot of companies aren't totally in touch with what their assets are. The penalties for not being in touch can be severe. American Express thought they were building on their assets and building a new asset when they launched their Optima card, a revolving credit card, as a companion to their traditional card/product line. The Optima cards were distributed indiscriminately to American Express cardholders. American Express took a huge bad debt write-off when Optima cardholders didn't pay their bills as swiftly as they did their American Express bill. Many didn't pay at all.

In an effort to get more cash, American Express management misread their assets:

1. Many of the American Express cards were paid by corporate accounts or were used for business. They were a business necessity and bills were paid expeditiously.
2. The American Express card is not a credit card. Cardmembers have to pay the whole bill on time or risk losing their privileges.

By misreading their research about their key strengths, American Express created dross.

Recognizing and exploiting assets to their utmost potential can create new markets for entrepreneurs or allow the entrepreneur to profit by riding the coattails of existing markets. Most of us in business, or even in our private lives, recognize the obvious assets or equities. These can be the gargantuan machinery, our creative people, or even the gobs of money to throw at business opportunities. Sometimes the other assets are harder to pinpoint. It's up to the entrepreneur or manager to recognize the equity that's ripe for exploitation or to build and exploit an asset where none seems to exists.

The four strategic basics to equity leveraging are to:

1. Identify
2. Segment

3. Focus
4. Attack

*Identify* new assets in your company and target new markets for your products. Pay particular attention to consumer-perceived value-added enhancements and of course, your brand assets. *Segment* your target products. Concentrate on those markets where you could have the strongest influence—the path of least consumer resistance. *Focus* your resources—product, sales, R&D—on fulfilling consumer needs in new ways to enhance the demand for these assets. *Attack* the marketplace with all the strength you can muster. Make it happen.

Management today often fails to recognize an asset or lets it go all too soon, before it starts paying a dividend. That's like owning land with giant oil reserves under it and using it to plant cabbage. Brand equity is one of the factors that acquirers look at when valuing a company. That's what A&W Beverages, based in New York, loves. A&W buys the dross of the soda industry—brands no one wants or cares about anymore, such as Vernors Ginger Ale and Squirt—and creates niche product opportunities from them.

The successful manager or entrepreneur ventures far beyond the boundaries of conventional wisdom for new-product positionings, new benefits, new niches, and new distribution systems and creates new assets.

The successful product developer creates new realities in the ever-changing marketplace instead of harping on the good old days. Some assets have to be recognized to be developed. Sometimes the assets are hard to find. We get so close to our product we have a blind spot. Or we simply get bored and don't believe in the uniqueness of our products anymore.

Assets don't usually come up to you, kick you in the behind, and scream "I'm an asset." You have to carefully probe your product, your company, and your consumers. That scourge of humanity—the preconceived notion, the accepted wisdom of the times—can hide your assets from you most efficiently or can paint an incorrect picture, like it did with American Express. Marketers can get too smart for themselves.

Building on "accepted wisdom" is like building on no foundation at all. For instance, most research is built on prior research that was carried out months or even years before. Or marketers rely on those ubiquitous and nefarious "housewives carrying clipboards" or past performances to get a reading on what will work today. Although every major manufacturer turned down toothpaste in a pump because it failed in the 1950s, Minnetonka defied accepted wisdom and created a new brand in an oral care category that was once seemingly impervious to new entrants.

There's a flip side to asset exploitation, the product negative. No product is perfect to everyone. All products are a series of tradeoffs to the developer and the end user. For every product benefit, there is a negative lurking. Failure to acknowledge and transform these negatives into assets can be disastrous. If you don't discover your negatives and compensate in some way your competitors surely will.

For IBM and Compaq computers, that negative was a certain stubbornness. Call it smugness if you will. IBM had a blind spot when it came to laptop computers. Inexplicably, they ignored the market, and Compaq computers rushed in where IBM would not tread. But then Compaq ran into trouble due to the same measure of hardheadedness that wounded IBM.

**Slice of Life**

Their notebook-sized machines, the COMPAQ LTE/286 and the COMPAQ LTE, were typical of the company itself. They were not flashy or brimming on the outside with technological sleight of hand but workhorses with a host of features and technological improvements under the covers—a foxy combination of state-of-the-art technology and market-driven mass appeal. Compaq's features quickly became the industry standard.

Here's when you have to know a little about Compaq's corporate culture. The people can be a little stubborn, or as they like to say, "disciplined." Compaq's discipline almost borders on self-flagellation. They had steadfastly refused to play the low-price game or sell to anyone outside their distribution chain. While most vendors have multiple channels of distribution, Compaq had only one, marketing exclusively through selected dealers (who also handled other lines), totally ignoring alternative distribution routes.

Competitors quickly knocked off the Compaq product, selling through the distribution avenues that Compaq tried to pretend didn't exist, and Compaq lost its major marketing advantages.

Negatives can be neutralized when we deal with them creatively. It's easy to sink into the morass of your problems. There are plenty of people who will help. "Misery loves company" is not only a cliché but a fact of life. The grass is always brown on your side of the fence if that's the way you choose to see it.

Ben B. Bliss, for over 40 years an authority on new product development and brand positioning, says that too many of the middle-management people are like horses in a dusty, sandy corral who have eaten all the grass. They poke their heads over the fence, looking at lush, green pastures, but keep going around in circles as a herd, fearful of going out through an open gate. Occasionally there is one horse that is more audacious and daring than the rest who goes out into the unknown. Of course, the herd follows behind.

To help you understand how to deal with potential negatives and how to accentuate your positives, here's a short course into the basic physical anatomy of the lowly chicken. No matter how advanced our knowledge of genetics has become, chickens are not born as skinless, boneless brown patties covered with bread crumbs. Nor are any varieties born with yellow skin. Actually, at one time, chickens were not considered lowly at all. They were an expensive meat served at special Sunday dinners. As factory farming came into its own, chicken production blossomed and prices plummeted. Chickens became a commodity, low-priced item for the dinner table. In short, they became a staple.

Of course, when goods become staples, the price plummets, and producers have to be content to run a volume enterprise. That's the accepted wisdom. But is it true? Is there no way to combat the negative of a commodity or—heavens!—a parity product?

**Slice of Life**

In all the books about marketing and the great brand names, you will rarely hear the name Frank Perdue mentioned in the same breath as Ivory Soap or Arm & Hammer. It should be. Mentioning the name Perdue without thinking of a chicken is like listening to the William Tell Overture without thinking of the Lone Ranger. Through sheer merchandising savvy, Perdue used his name to create an equity. I don't think it would be stretching the truth to say that he essentially created a new breed of chicken—the Perdue—not in the scientific way, but in the consumer's mind. He lifted his product out of the commodity hell-hole category it was in through the deft use of marketing and advertising. The characteristics of a Perdue chicken are hangtags and recipes on every bird, a yellow skin, and Frank Perdue as daddy of the flock.

Technically, most common breeds of chicken sold for consumption are the same, except, of course, Perdue chicken. Right? Perdue chicken must be different, the skin is yellow. Why is a yellow skin good? Because Frank Perdue said it was. Why does Perdue chicken have yellow skin? Because Perdue feeds his chickens pulverized marigold petals. Why are the nation's chicken producers always mad at Frank Perdue? Because they didn't think of it themselves. Perdue was the first branded and advertised chicken. The perceived value that Perdue added to the product had consumers flocking to the store, preferring to buy this "new" product over the multitude of similar chickens that hailed from mysterious and unknown origins. Perdue created the perception of quality and a noticeable point of difference in the consumer's mind.

He didn't do anything that you can't do for your own company using the four steps we outlined above. He *identified* his one big asset—himself—and created a larger-than-life persona about himself. He *segmented* his market by concentrating on those poultry buyers who were not price shoppers and who respected and responded to a brand name. He *focused* everything—all his media, promotion, point-of-sale, sales efforts, and even the color and size of his chickens—on communicating the stand-out persona. He *attacked* with the full force of his advertising budget the weakness of the existing "mystery" brands.

## The Word "Parity" Is a Value Judgment

One of the marketing person's most difficult and confusing dilemmas is building a share for a so-called parity product—one that has no apparent advantage over others in a category. Perdue said "no problem" and simply created an apparent product benefit when none really existed by taking stock of himself.

The key word is apparent. There is no such thing as a parity product or even a low-interest product as long as a consumer has to make a choice. Consumers must make a value judgment about each product they choose. My studies show they give your product about 16 seconds. Yet some products magically succeed in building and maintaining share dominance while others always seem to be continually playing follow the leader (which, as we mentioned, can still be profitable).

Watch a customer make a buying decision about a so-called parity product such as processed American cheese. Watch the customer pick up a package of cheese. Then put it down. Then pick it up. Then watch the customer compare labels and prices. To the customer there's a difference between identical products. If there is no difference, you can create one like Frank Perdue did and like we did with Deli Singles. Or you can create consumer-perceived enhancements for your product.

Consumer preference for young white chicken meat created another problem for the poultry industry. What could they do with hens that were no longer able to lay? These birds were older, tougher, and had an abundance of dark meat. McDonald's chicken suppliers had the answer. They cut and formed the chicken into tiny medallions, then coated them with bread crumbs. McDonald's added little packets of cloyingly sweet sauces and, voila!, Chicken McNuggets were created.

Tyson Foods, once strictly a poultry producer out of Springdale, Arkansas, now has sales of over $4 billion annually. Value-enhanced products—flavored, sliced, cooked, glazed, quick frozen items—now account for more than 85 percent of its sales.

## Coming Back from Disaster

Pitfalls are marketing problems waiting to be solved. No matter how bleak the outlook appears at the time, most corporate pitfalls are only temporary embarrassments, no matter how bleak they look at the time. In the dynamics of building an asset, a stumble has only transient consumer relevance. Consumers have short memories when it comes to product negatives. Suzuki weathered the storm over its side-rolling Samurais after an initial decrease in sales.

It's important to take the offensive, to continue to build your assets by creating bolder, more audacious initiatives. If you think your marketing problems are too difficult to overcome, think of the problems George Westinghouse created when he tried to market his new product—DC current—over Thomas Edison's competing AC current. His problem was one of life and death. Really. Prisons were using the Westinghouse current (with Edison's enthusiastic encouragement) to execute convicts "humanely" in the electric chair. Having your product associated with "death" is not a super positioning strategy. It doesn't do much for perceived value either or share of heart. But this perception was eventually overcome when Westinghouse used the current to illuminate the Chicago Columbian Exposition for six months. The fact that there was no injury helped restore faith in the system.

It's hard for some marketers to realize that the spoils often go not to the best product but to the best marketer of a product. It's not always advantageous to lead with your best product. Like Compaq discovered, if you're leading with your best shot, where do you go from there? It doesn't make a difference how many patents you have, someone is going to make a product better than yours. Maybe not better, but with a greater consumer-perceived value. In contrast, by taking stock of its key strengths, Kodak wisely concentrates on its film and name strengths, ceding most of the camera market to competitors. At one time, Osborne (computers), Kloss (projection TVs), and Sony (Betamax VCRs) had products that were superior to all other existing products and lost their franchise due to the heavy competition of the marketplace and failure to switch gears.

## Look at Your Product in a New Way

Products such as light bulbs, toilet paper, and aspirin are often referred to, in textbooks, as low-interest or low-involvement products. In reality, there are no low-interest products, only bored and out-of-touch marketers.

General Electric learned how to squeeze more usable light out of its light bulbs and initially marketed these Miser lights on the proposition of saving 5 watts of electricity out of each 100-watt bulb. Consumers were vitally uninterested. Although G.E. had this "can't miss" technology, consumers couldn't relate the benefits to their own lives. Since the energy savings were a miniscule portion of the utility bill, there was no visual cue and no value reinforcement.

G.E. then repositioned the bulb. Instead of energy saving, it said "more light for your money." That's a benefit that almost any consumer can relate to. The benefit reinforces itself every time the consumer turns on the light or when they get 70 watts of brightness from a 60-watt fixture.

Tell someone who needs it that toilet paper is a low-interest category.

## Opportunities from By-Products

Sometimes your by-products can be assets worth developing. American Airlines initially developed its sophisticated, state-of the-art Sabre reservations system for its own use. Demand became so great that they're offering it to competitors and travel agencies. Industry analysts think that Sabre is actually a more important profit center to American Airlines than American's flights.

The ultra successful Topp's collectors cards were another example of the tail wagging the dog. Baseball cards were originally packaged to help sell Topp's prime product—bubble gum. The bubble gum in the package kept shrinking as the card collecting hobby grew, spurred on by the graying of the baby boomers. Topp's recently completed the cycle: They eliminated the gum completely.

## Opportunities from Golden Oldies

In the continual search for new products, the big marketing opportunity might be the product you've been ignoring all these years, that is if you can forget the self-fulfilling prophecy called the "product life cycle." A more destructive theory has never been put forth. According to this theory, the average product goes through humanlike life phases—birth, growth, maturity, death. But we've all seen spry, agile people of 80 and we've all seen dull, lifeless people in their 20s.

Products don't die. They are killed by neglect. The only life cycle is in the interest shown to the brand or product by its marketers. In a typical scenario, the brand managers and company management have simply missed the opportunity to evolve the product to fit changing lifestyles or new competitive situations.

For instance, despite the major changes in media, today's younger homemakers often want what their grandmothers had. Certain of grandmother's products have an involvement with consumers that transcends reason. Like furniture, some products have taken on a patina with age. Murphy's soap is one example of a product in this category. It's an older product originally made by a guy who decided to turn his oil into soap (I can't decide if that makes him a genius or not). It's inconvenient. It's messy. It's oily. And almost any consumer research study would say the product has no relevance in today's spray-it-on, wipe-it-off world. Yet consumers swear by it. Like others of grandmother's products, consumers have attached mythical powers of strength and effectiveness that have grown with the passage of time.

When selecting a candidate for revitalization, it's important to skip a generation. Consumers still have unresolved conflicts with good old mom and dad. But everyone loves grandma. Her house was always spotless. Her meals were the ultimate in nutrition. She was strength personified.

As in the marketing of all consumer goods, consumer perceptions are the only thing. Perceptions are much more important than reality. Consumers feel that many new products have secretly had the effectiveness taken out of them. They feel that there is less of the active ingredients.

When advertising and marketing the older product, it's important not to spend your advertising and promotional dollars harkening back to the product's age. The age of the product should speak for itself, through word of mouth and through visual packaging signals. You must stress the product benefits to allow consumers to rationalize the purchase. Murphy talks about strength and versatility. Arm & Hammer offers the perception of purity and strength. Advertising the known Arm & Hammer heritage would be a waste of time and money.

**Teach Your Older Product a New Trick.** Attach new uses to your product. Consumers love to discover new ways for the tried and true. New fabrics, new home surfaces, new ways of eating all provide new repositioning for old reliables.

**Choose Your Candidates Selectively.** The younger old products (from the ancient period of the 1960s and late 1950s) need more emotional fine tuning. The 1960s product has an identity crisis. Not old enough to take on mythological proportions, not new enough to be perceived as modern and exciting.

**Brand Opportunities Are Unlimited.** Esquire shoe polish. Kiwi shoe polish. Fels Naptha soap. Uneeda biscuits. You could look at them in two ways. As tired old products, or as marketing classics, always gaining a new audience. Take advantage of these classics. The old-style logo should be prominently featured on the package, in the ads, in the promotion. Don't fall into the fatal flaw of becoming bored with your older brands. They can be so old, they're new.

Today's love of Grandma's things may be a rebellion against all the choices offered in the store. They may represent a back-to-basics simplicity and a reinforcement to consumers that their purchase was a smart one. Capitalize on your marketing classics. They're difficult to create; they have to evolve in their own way. That's the nature of a classic.

## Recovering from Mistakes

Unlike the oldtime chemists who played at turning dross into gold, you can do it when you stay focused and upbeat. Follow these guidelines:

- If something goes wrong, don't spend money or time on "why it went wrong" studies to figure out where you goofed. They're a waste. Learn how to do it right, through experimentation and research.
- Constantly monitor your market for any kind of sales change. Talk to the consumer before things get out of hand.
- Keep coming up with knowledge you didn't know before by researching and probing.
- Try a relaunch before you declare a product dead. Try a new name. A new image. A new pricing structure. Don't take anything for granted. Your competitors sure won't.

Consumers are dealing with a different set of values than the marketer. Where the marketer is concerned with what can be put into the product to get a competitive edge, the consumer is saying, "What's in it for me?" Constant experimentation is the key to keeping your products vibrant and alive.

## Other Assets

Other assets you may be overlooking include:

1. *Brand image value.* What are consumers looking at when they buy your brand? Are there certain tangibles or intangibles that can lead to a quick new product success?
2. *Licensing.* Perhaps your name is the most important asset you have. Try it on new products and perhaps other companies will buy the uses of your name to help them in their business.

3. *Existing sales organization or distribution system.* Sometimes a distribution systems is so strong that you can piggy back other products on it. For instance, Frito-Lay has outstanding (and expensive) route distribution systems. It may be ideal for other for other companies to ride the Frito-Lay saleswagon to get fresh baked goods into the store.
4. *Formulas.* It goes without saying that sometimes a company's greatest asset is the secret formula for a product hidden away in a safe. Nobody has ever been able to duplicate the textures and tastes of Thomas' english muffins and Thomas has developed new offshoots of their product that have stayed proprietary.
5. *Patents or technology.* You may be able to do something that no one else can do without spending tons of money. You can either license or sell the patent or technology and make extra income.
6. *Available plant capacity.* Although many companies shy away from this, creating private label products or off brands can fill out your line or make sure that you are flanking your own products on all price points on the shelves. Private labeling also gives the consumer a benchmark reference point on the quality of a product in a given category. It might even provide a profitable outlet on your factory seconds or products that are not up to your usual high standards.

To the aware new product development person, almost nothing is without a buyer somewhere. Would you believe bat guano, mined (if that's the right word for it) from the caverns of New Mexico is an effective and expensive fertilizer? Mesquite, the wood we use to give our barbecue added zing, is nothing but a (formerly) useless weed that grows in the Southwest. Jack Daniel's distillery in Tennessee sells the wood that's left over from their charcoal filtering process as pricey charcoal briquets.

## Summary

1. It's easy to fall into the morass of your problems. It's not too difficult to sell a cure for cancer, but, unfortunately, most products aren't like that. The important thing is to recognize your strong points and to build on them.
2. Very often a problem is an opportunity waiting to be exploited.
3. Know thyself is a key to growing your assets and your business.

## Questions, Answers, and Additional Insights

*I would like to revitalize an older product, but I'm afraid that the product can't cut it in today's world. Other products have surpassed it in effectiveness.*
Put the old name on a new product. You probably couldn't afford to pay for all the goodwill that's locked up in that grand old name. Use the new product for effectiveness and the old name to build credibility. It's important to work with consumers to find out how meaningful the product name really is to them. Consumers have a tremendous loyalty to brand names and will try a product they know and trust. It's silly and even heartbreaking to throw all that brand equity away, sort of like granny-dumping.

*How do I find out how strong my brand equity is?*
Place the brand name you want to evaluate on ads, concepts, and even packages of competing similar products. If your brand name makes consumers prefer your product above the competition's product, than you have a winner. By asking questions about what the name means, how memorable it is, and the strengths or negatives, you'll quickly ascertain leveragability.

*Help, I've got a Sixty Minutes sound crew at my door, Consumers Reports said my product was lousy, and I think my product contributes to high cholesterol.... Do I just close up shop?*
Disaster management, or damage control, is big business, and with good reason. A media crash can make your sales crash in a hurry. The good news is that although they can be painful to deal with, disasters can be forgotten quickly. Long-term consumer effects are often negligible unless consumers expect the accident to affect them directly. Most corporate disasters are examples of transient consumer relevance. Although the usual reaction against media is to get defensive, it's not good strategy. Don't cover up; don't lash out at the media: Attacking the media falls into the "When did you stop beating your wife?" category. You can't win. Listen to your consumers. Find out how deeply aware of the problem they were and develop your strategy with a good offense. For instance, when consumers perceived that tropical oils were raising cholesterol, the smart marketers removed it from their product and advertised "No Tropical Oils" as if they never had them to begin with. Deal with the problem on a positive, creative basis, and sales will eventually return. Don't reinforce the situation by braying that it's not true. Your message will never get through and you'll only succeed in reinforcing the negative media feeding frenzy.

# 11
# Selling Out

*Chapter preview:*

- ***What to do before you sell***
- ***The pros and cons of selling out***
- ***What acquiring companies are looking for***
- ***Writing the ideal "pitch" letter***
- ***How to create the ideal impression***
- ***Why companies run like hell from the unsolicited idea, and how to make them run to you***
- ***Ammunition and requisites for the sales pitch***

This chapter is about a practical method of getting your business bought out, provided that this is the road you want to take. Selling out may not be for everybody, but judging from the phone calls I get in my office, it seems like that's what everyone wants. The least common denominator of the people who call requesting marketing help is that they all want to know how to be bought out by a large company. In the 1960s and 1970s, selling out was a goal to be avoided. Now it's a goal in itself.

It's intriguing that when entrepreneurs request marketing or advertising help, they usually ask what the fee is. When they ask me for introductions to my corporate clients, they offer me a percentage, payable, of course, only when the deal is done.

Interestingly, most corporations are actively looking for businesses to acquire—not to the extent they were before they started paying off the junk bonds—but they are always interested in new ways to increase their business with the least amount of effort. Buying an existing equity or acquiring a new brand name is a hassle-free way of accomplishing this. One of the reasons corporations have to do this is because their own new product programs fall far short of their goals. They're forced to acquire rather than create.

The key to positioning your product or business as an acquisition candidate can be paraphrased by the mystical voice in the hit movie *Field of Dreams:* "Build it and they will come."

The major mistake marketers make is having nothing to sell and selling it very badly. As we mentioned earlier, coming up with the idea is simple; even producing it is a snap compared with selling it to another company.

For the most part companies don't want to buy ideas or even products. They want businesses. They want opportunities they can build on—short cuts to new markets and profits. If you want to sell your product to a company and get the most out of the deal, you should sell first to the consumer and build a demonstrable sales base.

The more functional and focused your business is, the easier it will be to sell. Acquiring companies want to fit a business opportunity into their ongoing methods and systems as simply as possible. If they sell to frozen food departments and the acquirer's trucks are equipped with freezers, they're usually not interested in dairy case or refrigerated products. In your eyes they might have tunnel vision, but it's their business and their tunnel, so you just have to deal with it.

Companies are also not interested in raw ideas; they're inundated with them (although working prototypes with a strong success potential may be welcomed). My experience has shown that most companies run like hell from unsolicited ideas. They consider them nuisances. Many companies won't even look at ideas for fear of being sued if they come up with a similar idea on their own. The new-products director of a prestigious consumer medical product company relates how he gets suggestions for developing a tannish brown bandage for the African American market or people with dark skins every month.

## Selling a Business Takes Nerves of Steel and Maalox

Selling a product or business to another company is like trying to catch a tiny butterfly. You think you have it, but when you open your hand, it's not there. Selling a business can be an exercise in frustration because you're dealing with so many human elements beyond your control.

### Slice of Life

Recently, we received a missive from our client, a major financial company (the acquirer). It was about to enter a relationship (a buy-out) with a provider of travel services (the acquiree). We were asked to position the travel company within the financial service company and to ascertain the synergy between the two businesses. The acquisition looked promising and rewarding for both sides. We had several meetings with our client and several meetings with the candidate. The candidate was tremendously excited—after five years he was about to go big time. Then it happened—more the usual than the rarity—the department of the financial services company that had initiated the acquisition was reorganized. The two corporate sponsors of the deal were transferred into new positions.

The buyout fell through because the new people coming in had no knowledge of the deal and, of course, different agendas. A switch in management almost always results in slow down or elimination of acquisition plans.

Selling your business is where these clichés come to play:

- It's not over till the fat lady sings.
- It ain't over until it's over.
- Count on nothing but your fingers (or until the check clears the bank).

But businesses and prototypes are being acquired regularly. You can make it happen, provided you really want to invest the time and have the fortitude to see it through.

Should you be selling out in the first place? Let's look at the good points and the not-so-good points. The good points are:

1. You'll probably make money. More if it's an ongoing business, considerably less if your product is only in the prototype phase. Although a functioning business can be valued by basic accounting methods (as well as intangible equities such as brand names or proprietary formulas and patents), a prototype venture is much more speculative. In the latter case, the entrepreneur typically receives a small advance or cash award, plus 2 to 5 percent of gross or net sales for a predetermined period. All this is negotiable. Small percentages, or "points," can add up to a substantial, ongoing source of income.
2. You may be able to license part of your business and keep the rest. You might sell a special name or patent and still keep control over your rights.
3. You may have no interest or lack the resources to develop and market the product on your own.
4. You may be the type of person for whom developing the business is more fun than the ongoing daily struggles of keeping it operating in the black.
5. Playing with other people's money is a lot more desirable than using your own.
6. Their assets and resources may be stronger than your own and may increase the market of your product.

Not-so-good points about selling out are:

1. It's your baby after all—the product you brought forth and slowly nurtured. If you sell, you're going to lose control. If you sell and stay on in some capacity, you'll go crazy when the new owners do things differently than you. They might even change the product in some untoward way. Even if your business has not been particularly or consistently financially rewarding, post partum blues will definitely and sometimes devastatingly take their toll.
2. You may not make a great deal of money. In fact, you probably won't make as much money as the business magazines would expect you to believe (but your friends will think you did, so it's almost the same), especially if you have a prototype or licensing arrangement and the acquiring company is either slow or lax in developing or promoting your product. Perhaps new management will come in and shelve your product permanently. You may make nothing except your advance. Nada. Zilch.
3. Your kids will probably never be able to enter the family business.
4. The buying company (if they did their homework) will probably make more money than you. If you're the jealous type, this carries more weight than you might expect.
5. Now, what do you do with your life? If you're like most entrepreneurs, this venture has probably occupied your days and your nights. Undoubtedly, you're going to have some kind of withdrawal symptoms after the initial euphoria wears off, and you'll feel a certain aimlessness. (You'll probably leap into the fray with another new product again or try to become a new product consultant.)

## Before You Attempt to Sell

*Do your homework.* Invariably, because entrepreneurs have less money than they need, especially if their sole product is a prototype, they eliminate the necessary consumer research, expecting the prospective company to provide it. They usually won't. Besides the monetary considerations, conducting your own research gives you an advantage. You control the research function instead of leaving it to others, who don't understand your product, to foul up.

Quality research—focus groups or one-on-ones—will point out misguided marketing plans so you can fix them before the acquiring company discovers them. Research can also score points with the potential acquirer by supplying the key consumer information you'll need for your pitch. If you're really sure of your product, you can even invite your prospective suitor to your groups.

Put the acquiring company's name on your package and the company will be delighted with the consumer response to *their* new product. The best presenter in the world can't elicit the feelings the acquirer gets when prospective consumers cheer for their new product.

Even a less-than-optimum consumer response can help the sale, as we discovered in focus groups for our medical product. Surgeons spent two hours disparaging our concept and prototypes. Very depressing. But after that humiliation, we demonstrated the product to a group of nurses, who turned out to be major influencers in the hospital purchasing decision. The four hours spent in the focus room represented a microcosm of our target market and made us and our product more credible to our prospective suitor.

If you're forthright in dealing with the acquirer, they may even pay to help you do your research.

*Create a business plan,* geared for the company you are trying to sell to. It must include:

Who you are

Where you are

Where you are going

How you can get there

Most important, what it's going to do for the acquirer

*Get your product into the consumer's hands.* Build a track record. Create demand for your product. Companies like nothing more than to buy what's already selling. If supermarkets are too difficult, try the mom-and-pop stores. Sell at flea markets and fairs. The important things are to build a sales base and debug your product before the final pitch.

*Research the companies you want to sell to.* How will your product fit into the company's lines? What are you bringing to the game? How receptive are they to new products? What is their track record? Why should they deal with you? Make sure you sell the company the dream, but tinge it with reality. Define your target market. The most important question is whether the acquirer will spend money and time making it work.

Obtain the potential acquirer's annual report. Obtain the reports of competing companies. Compare them thoroughly to position your company and services.

## Where Do You Find Prospects?

Unfortunately there is no single source that will tell you who and how you should target your product offering (although I had considered writing one) and what various companies are interested in acquiring, so you are left to your own devices. Here are some starting points:

- *The supermarket.* Explore products in the supermarket or department store. How would your product fit into a company's existing product line? Where are they lacking? Can a product be made on the acquirer's existing factory lines? Perhaps a company would like to piggy-back your product in their own distribution system. That's one of the reasons Frito-Lay bought Smartfood. Sales and distribution systems meshed perfectly with Frito-Lay's own systems.
- *Trade associations/trade shows.* Trade associations can be marvelous sources of help for an entrepreneur. The associations' business is helping members increase profits and product lines. Almost every library has a source book of associations that will often give the size of the company and the key people. Trade shows are also a strong source of generating leads. They can be your trade shows or the acquiring company's shows, because almost all attendees are looking to expand a business in one manner or another.
- *Media.* Media people are my first stop. They know everything. It's their job. Recently a company asked me to help them market a cargo retainer for trucks. My very first step was call the editor of an automotive trade magazine. He gave me the name of a Truck Part Distributors Association, which (for a miniscule fee) sent me a directory of every truck part distributor in my area. If you ask nicely, most editors will send you a free issue of their magazine, where you can get more leads.
- *The Standard Directory of Advertisers.* Most libraries will have this book. It gives you a rundown on who owns what product and trade name and how much the listed companies spend on advertising. It will also give you the names and titles of people to contact. I make this book an important part of my searches, because one can often gauge a company's aggressiveness by what they spend on advertising. Other important directories are Dun and Bradstreets' list of corporations and the Thomas Register.
- *Make friends with your librarian.* This person is an underrated source of tremendous help. The librarian undoubtedly will have directories you need or will help you obtain them. Many libraries now have computerized periodical retrieval systems. Simply key in the area you need and a listing of important articles about your business or product will be found. It's an easy, productive way to generate leads and to learn more about your market.

By the way, since we are talking about resources, one area to stay away from is the alleged invention marketing services. They usually can't supply any information you can't get yourself, but they charge you enough for you to think you might be getting something. They're akin to the vanity presses in the publishing industry. A vanity press will publish your book for a fee. These invention companies will do a snow job on your ego but lead you down the road to nowhere—for a fee.

## Prospecting for Gold with Paper and a Phone

Once you've refined your prospect list, how do you make your approach? Unless you already have an "in" to the company, you usually have two methods. The phone and the mail. They say letter writing is a lost art. It's a shame, because a good letter serves as your résumé and your recommendation.

Many companies have standard rules and procedures to follow for presenting a product or idea. Ignore these rules. You don't get points for following directions in the real world. Go to the president first. The president is usually the one who is most open to new ideas. New-business divisions and engineering departments can only get in your way because of the dread NIH (Not Invented Here) Syndrome. Speaking to these people is often like a dialog through a one-way mirror. You can see them, but they can only see themselves.

Earlier we said that the entrepreneur's most vital assets are a computer or typewriter and a list of people. It's even more essential when looking for an acquirer. Your preliminary contact can be through letter or a phone call. Write a letter to the president of the company or call directly. Tell presidents just enough about the product and how it is going to help their companies to pique their interest. The best time to get to presidents are before 8:00 or 9:00 in the morning or after 5:00 or 6:00 in the evening.

This is how we went about generating interest in our medical product: After ascertaining the president's interest on the phone, I found that he had been involved with joint ventures before. I followed up with this letter (names have been changed):

Dear Mr. Smith:

It was a pleasure speaking with you today. As we discussed, we are interested in entering into a joint venture with a textile manufacturer to develop a product for the health care industry. We are currently developing specifications and prototypes as well as doing informal market research.

As background information about my company, New Products Workshop develops new products, product positionings, and marketing strategy for major companies. Our clients include Pepsico, Colgate-Palmolive, The Wool Bureau, Arm & Hammer, Kraft, American Express, Ralston-Purina, and American Cyanamid.

We've helped develop Glad Lock Storage bags, Cocktails for Two for Schenley, and Kibbles & Chunks and Lucky Dog pet foods for Ralston-Purina. We opened up a major new profit category for Colgate and were responsible for the worldwide repositioning of a famous Pepsi soft drink—to name a few successes.

I also write regular features for marketing magazines about new products and marketing. We should meet to discuss this joint opportunity.

Sincerely,

Barry Feig
President

The letter accomplished several things:

- Short, sweet, and to the point, it became a physical entity that could be passed around to others in the organization.
- It whetted the prospect's appetite to hear more.
- The short list of accomplishments established my credibility.
- The research paragraph showed him we were serious about our business.
- The last sentence, while an action sentence, left both of us room to maneuver in terms of dates and places.

Now, you're probably saying that you don't have a background like mine. It doesn't matter. Everyone has an asset of some kind that they can exploit. The important thing is to establish credibility and not come off as some kind of crackpot. Your asset may be the length of time you've been in business, special school degrees, or how the product is currently being received by the consumer.

All letters should be followed by a phone call to spur the project onward. Always present new stimuli for the prospect to react to. Always show progress. It's essential to make it look like everything's moving forward at all times.

After receiving a positive response, we went further.

August 4, 1989

Dear Mr. Smith:

We're looking forward to meeting with you in New York on

September 13 at 11:00. We know our unique product story will intrigue you. We'd appreciate your signing and returning the attached confidentiality agreement. If you have any questions, please call me.

Sincerely,

Barry Feig
President

A word about confidentiality agreements. They can be short or long. There is always the standard paranoia among entrepreneurs that an idea will be stolen. While I haven't seen an outright theft when dealing with a major company, it doesn't hurt to take precautions. After all, just because you're paranoid, it doesn't mean that nobody is following you. Don't show anything to anyone without your confidentiality agreement in hand. If a company balks, run.

Here's an agreement we use. *Disclaimer:* I drew up this confidentiality statement myself, without the aid of a lawyer. Use it strictly at your own risk. I make no claims whatsoever about its thoroughness and suitability for the purposes you may intend. A visit to the library will offer other "boilerplate" formats that you can adapt.

Dear Mr. Smith:

As a preliminary step to entering into a possible joint venture between ABC Company and New Products Workshop, Inc., it is agreed New Products Workshop, Inc. will make available certain plans, goals, programs, research, financial projections, technical data, and product prototypes which are deemed to be "confidential information."

In consideration of such disclosure, ABC Company agrees that it shall not use such confidential information for any purpose other than that contemplated by this agreement.

| ABC Company | New Products Workshop, Inc. |
|---|---|
| By: ______________________ | By: ______________________ |
| Title: ______________________ | Title: ______________________ |
| Date: ______________________ | Date: ______________________ |

### Getting Past the Secretary

Undoubtedly you'll run across the well-meaning but protective secretary who seems to thwart your every move. Unless you can convince the secretary of the importance of your call, you efforts may be for nil. Fortunately there are many techniques for getting through:

- *Pronounce the prospect's name correctly.* An incorrect pronunciation is a red flag that you are an unknown caller and are probably trying to sell something. If you're not sure, ask the person at the switchboard.
- *Get the secretary's name.* Just asking the secretary for a name helps build a more communicative and less formal relationship.
- *After the initial call, use the prospect's first name.* It sounds to the secretary like you may have already begun a relationship.
- *Don't ask to be put through. State it as if it were a foregone conclusion.* Be authoritative but polite. Be polite but persistent.
- *Don't ask the prospect to call you.* You'll lose the freedom of action, and even if the prospect does (and the prospect probably won't), you won't be as prepared as you might be if you generated the call. Ask, as a direct question, when would be a good time to call and follow up as promised.
- *Call before 9:00 and after 5:00.* Usually the prospect will get his or her own phone and will have to talk.
- *Sell the secretary in one or two sentences but only if you're backed into a corner.* More often than occasionally, the secretary won't let you past the gate unless you say exactly what you want. Keep it short. Don't depend on the secretary to do your selling for you.

## The Pitch

There are as many theories about what makes a proper presentation as there are new products on the shelf. One rule that must be followed is always bring an extra bulb for the slide projector. The second rule is always speak to your audience's needs. They're interested in what you can bring to their table.

Some people prefer heavy dramatics, some like dog-and-pony shows, some simply come in with their product and some notes and talk. All work as long as you have a story to tell and dreams to sell. One thing is certain though—you almost always have just one chance, so you had better give it your best shot. Whether you use charts, slides, or acetate overheads, always be prepared.

Every pitch should be specially tailored to the company you're presenting to. While this may seem like standard operating procedure, novice entrepreneurs tend to be more excited about the meeting itself than the ultimate goal, which is to sell your product. You don't want to become a professional visitor.

You should have with you the following:

- Prototypes or actual products with the prospect's logo on the product or package and backups to keep Murphy (of Murphy's law) happy.
- Ads for the product or comprehensive roughs with selling benefits. Put the acquirer's name on the ads. As in the real world, an ad is the quickest way to get product benefits across.
- A short history of how the product came about.
- Sales figures or anticipated sales figures.
- Complete reasons that the product would fit into your prospect's company with a minimum of hassle.
- Knowledge of the prospect's business, sales, selling chain, and competitors—most of this information can come from the annual report or adept questioning at the beginning of the meeting.
- Expenses involved.
- A leave-behind that stresses the key points you just made.
- Next steps.

You are not selling a product but are selling an opportunity for the company. Don't ask the acquirer to do your thinking for you. Allow the audience an opportunity to react.

## Four Steps to a Successful Presentation

1. *The introduction.* Most entrepreneurs are very comfortable with the product and services they offer and immediately take out their product. That's wrong. Remember, in our visit to the time-share resort, the salesperson didn't show you the actual property until the salesperson was thoroughly familiar with your needs. Don't show your product until you have properly stated the prospect's case.

Ask pertinent and probing questions. The first minutes should be friendly, unassuming questions about the client's business. Ask questions about sales, competitors, distribution patterns, and even what areas the company is lacking. Some companies are more open about this than others. Some interviewers stare silently and nod once or twice. It's the answers to these questions that can make the vital difference between selling and showing.

Try to ascertain how the purchase decision is to be made. Who are the major players, the decision makers? Of course, if you're lucky enough to have the president at the meeting, then that part is done. Most groups will be divided into decision makers, secondary managers, technical people, and salespeople. All these groups will have different priorities and agendas.

2. *Now it's time for the pitch.* There are three major rules for any presentation:

- Tell them what you're going to tell them.
- Tell them.
- Then tell them what you told them.

Demonstrate the product and what it can mean to the company. Show photos of the product in use. Direct everything about the product into how it can help the prospect accomplish the goals of greater sales or new markets with a minimum of risk.

Talk specifics. General benefits are not as strong as specifics. How you position yourself to the company is as important as positioning the product to the consumer. The more specific you can make the benefit, the more effective it is. Discuss:

- Your target market
- Why your product is better than anyone else's
- Sales history
- Technology that is nonsecret

When you have identified a concern, the well-presented benefit can create genuine excitement. Financial payoffs are usually the most important benefits. They create the most interest.

3. *The summing up.* Open the floor to questions. If there are no questions, then the prospect is usually not interested.

4. *The finish.* Get a reaction from the prospects and outline next steps. Leave behind a handout that is clean and neat and that will keep the prospect excited.

## Follow-Ups

Keep the deal alive, at least in your mind. Having "deals" in progress helps with emotional gratification and keeps the adrenaline flowing.

Send a letter keeping the client up to date. If you have received no response, follow-up calls asking if the prospects have any questions can be helpful. It will also help you gauge how successful the presentation was.

Some additional steps to successful presentations include:

1. Use visual aids. You can choose between slides, overhead transparencies, flip charts, or artboards. All can be useful and all have trade-offs of one kind or another. Slides can be impressive, but they tend to inhibit spontaneity. They are more formal and the room must be dark. Acetate overheads can look tacky and dull. Although I find them a distraction, they can be effective in showing charts and graphs. Professionally lettered boards or flip charts give you the utmost flexibility. You can change or even stop your presentation as major points are raised.
2. Keep your presentation short and to the point. About 45 minutes should be more than sufficient. Extra time should be taken up by the prospect's questions.
3. Get your whole management team involved and state their purpose for attending the meeting at the outset. Prospects are suspicious of having people in the room whose roles are unknown.

## An Alternative to Selling Out

Perhaps you can't get a bite, then what? An alternative and far simpler route to take might be a strategic alliance with a supplier or acquirer. A strategic alliance is simply an arrangement between different companies (usually a large company and a smaller one) to merge equities in favor of a synergy to create even larger sales. It can mean gaining access to new distribution avenues, greater funding, and advertising and marketing support.

A client of mine had a proprietary system of dispensing beverages which he was going to license to beverage companies. One of his suppliers, a container company, was so entranced with the product and the long-range potential that he gave my client leads and introductions throughout the industry and eventually acquired the company itself. Once again, it's important to recognize your assets and your weaknesses so you can seek out an alliance that works for you and your "partner."

So now we've gone full circle. We've created a successful product. We've sold out and are now tinkering around the house, taking our much needed vacation. But despite the hassles and the sleepless nights we're probably going to start the whole damn thing again. Why? Because we're entrepreneurs. And that's what we do.

## Summary

1. The key to selling a business is to create a window of opportunity for an acquirer that the acquirer can't turn down.
2. The key to a successful presentation is a steady flow of communications, constantly stressing what's important for the acquiring company.
3. An alternative to selling out is forming strategic alliances that build on the key strengths of the "company partners."

## Questions, Answers, and Additional Insights

*Where should the selling presentation be made?*
There are three alternatives—your place, the client's place, or a neutral place, such as a hotel. Your place is best because you can control all the circumstances. This gives the prospect the chance to see your facilities and meet your people.

*How much can I really expect to make when I sell a prototype or a licensing arrangement?*
Every deal is 100 percent different: 2 to 5 percent of sales is usually a reasonable figure. Your banker or a competent patent attorney will probably be able to guide you toward setting a price.

# 12
# Before You Launch

*Chapter preview:*

- ***How to avoid the big mistake***
- ***How to make sure you're absolutely, positively ready for success***
- ***A note of encouragement***

A famous HBA company spent five years developing a new applicator. R&D was in ecstasy when it was perfected. But they forgot one thing. They didn't have a product to put into the state-of-the-art dispenser.

An entrepreneur (who had a great deal of success in other fields) had a dramatic new idea for a vodka. He had the name, the product, and a unique price structure and positioning. Trouble was the BATF (Bureau of Alcohol, Tobacco and Firearms) wouldn't approve his label, which short-circuited all his grandiose marketing plans.

Seven-Up spent several million dollars in advertising and manufacturing 7-Up Gold. Nobody cared. It died on the shelves instantaneously.

There is always an element of risk in developing new product. If new-product development were easy, everyone would do it. As the marketing vice president of a health and beauty aids company told me, "Barry, I have 12 inches of research on two new products that swore they were going to be successes. One made it, one didn't. How do you figure out which to go with?"

The recent recession has done a great deal of psychological damage to entrepreneurs. Plans have been stifled for lack of funding. The American dream of creating a new product has gone on hold, and fear has taken hold of the marketplace. Potential new-product developers are being stifled by gloom-and-doomers who shout "now is not the time."

But, as we mentioned earlier, birthing a new product is a lot like having your first child. If you wait for when you can really afford it, and for just the right time, you'll never have it. Fear breeds inertia, which breeds further inertia.

Think you're ready for the market? As someone said, half of knowledge is knowing where to find it, and hopefully this book has given you the knowledge you need to grow a business. You are your best asset, and learning about your market is the best use you can make of yourself.

Nobody ever sets out to create a market failure. Many errors can be avoided if you spend just 10 minutes stepping away from your product and looking at it objectively from as far away as your desk. New marketing segmentations and, of course, new consumer choices make any process inaccurate that is not evolutionary.

Here are some final questions to answer to make sure the odds of success are on your side.

1. *What will the competition do?* Although figuring out what the competition will do is a little like playing Nostradamus, if you've been doing your homework and are exploring the market constantly, you should have a pretty good idea of your competition's ultimate eruptions. If you have created a breakthrough product and are creating a major business, the competition is sure to notice and will probably react one of three ways, depending on its history:

- It will knock off your product and possibly add additional features.
- It will undercut you in price or short-term retail deals.
- It will spend heavily on advertising to blunt the effect of your product's impact.

2. *Does the product have a strong positioning and benefit?* Could you describe it in a sentence or less? Can the entire product story fit on a single page? The product positioning is the single most important part of the product benefits mix. Who is the product for? Why would this target market want it? What is the major benefit (physical or psychological)? How is it going to make a consumer's life better?

The positioning of a new product is much too important to leave to your advertising agency. The positioning of the product should be determined before it goes to the advertising agency. Despite what your agency says, if you don't bring them the positioning, they're just guessing. Can you afford it?

3. *Is there room to be creative with your pricing? Is your pricing strategy realistic? Can you make money on it?* The easiest way to price your product is at rock-bottom levels, but such pricing is not always the most advantageous. Pricing too low is as much of a sin as pricing too high. It's too easy to be locked in. If you find you priced your product too low, it can be difficult to deal or increase your prices. You can always come down in pricing, but it can be difficult to go up. Despite what consumers say, it's a rare product that lives or dies on price alone. Consumers will find the money if the product attracts them enough.

4. *Are all product performance cues reinforced? Does it work or taste as well as you promised it would?* Any good new product should sell itself four times: on the shelf, at the checkout, in use, and after it's used up it should leave the consumer wanting more. Unfortunately the prime example of this is the marketing of cigarettes, called the greatest consumer product ever made.

5. *Does the final product come close to the idea you originally had?* With all the necessary compromises that go into developing a new product, it's easy to lose our way. That's why it's always important to keep the spirit of the product in mind and, of course, the positioning. Constantly refer to your one-page product profile.

6. *Is there a product like this on the market?* Is it successful, or does it need the fine tuning that you can provide to make it successful? You'll invariably find it easier to grab on to a trend than to start a new one. Sell what's selling.

7. *Do you have a follow-up product in the hopper?* Your encores should be planned in advance. You should be working on your next ideas even before the first one is marketed. When the novelty and applause for your product wears off, people will want to see what you have next. (It's also easier to sell an idea to management or to money people if you can demonstrate the potential of future products.)

8. *Are you satisfied with the consumer responses? Really? Did you elicit negativity and deal with it in a positive way?* Would you show this product to a group of unknown consumers in front of your banker or your boss? When doing focus groups, a negative response is better than no response at all or a lackluster approval. This consumer work should have provided you with the raw material and enthusiasm to get the product into the supermarket.

9. *Is the name memorable?* While having a unique name for a product can be overrated, having a name that breaks out of the standard mold can elicit trial and provide a unique share of heart.

10. *Are you legal?* More than one product has bitten the dust because some obscure legal regulation has not been complied with. While I'm not a big fan of lawyers, they can help you through such things as trademark hurdles and legal clearances. Consultants can also help you clear the way through labyrinthine bureaucracies. It's advisable to get clearances way before you're ready to hit the market.

11. *Would you buy the product?* Is it something you would be proud to use at home or give to friends? Would you spend your own money on it?

## A Note of Encouragement

No book can claim to be the only source of new-product development because no book can replace the one factor that's vital to the new-product development process: You. New-product development is crazy, scary, and thrilling as we venture out into worlds where no one has ever gone before.

Four key requisites for a new-product development person to have are:

1. *Objectivity*—to see your product from the consumer's eyes and not from the vantage point of your own ego.
2. *Vision*—to grow with your product and your business to take them to unforeseen heights.
3. *Audacity*—to find and explore ideas when no one else is willing or everyone is laughing.
4. *Sensitivity*—to explore the nuances of the consumer mind with a questioning mind. For without a questioning mind, the other requisites are valueless.

Go for it! There's a world of opportunity out there.

# Company, Product, and Name Index

# Subject Index

## About the Author

Barry Feig has been developing new products and marketing opportunities for more than 20 years. He is president of New Products Workshop, Inc., a firm that helps large corporations and small entrepreneurial ventures develop new products and marketing strategies. His strategies and products for clients like American Express, Colgate-Palmolive, Pepsico, American Cyanamid, and Schenley Distillers have surpassed $2 billion in sales. Feig is the author of more than 50 articles on marketing, some of which have been published in *Advertising Age* and *American Demographics*. He currently writes a monthly column called "New Product Strategies" for *Food and Beverage Marketing*.